T0361280

Cambridge Elements ≡

Elements in Psychology and Culture
edited by
Kenneth Keith
University of San Diego

GENE–CULTURE INTERACTIONS

Toward an Explanatory Framework

Heewon Kwon
University of Hawaii at Manoa

Joni Y. Sasaki
University of Hawaii at Manoa

CAMBRIDGE
UNIVERSITY PRESS

CAMBRIDGE
UNIVERSITY PRESS

University Printing House, Cambridge CB2 8BS, United Kingdom

One Liberty Plaza, 20th Floor, New York, NY 10006, USA

477 Williamstown Road, Port Melbourne, VIC 3207, Australia

314–321, 3rd Floor, Plot 3, Splendor Forum, Jasola District Centre, New Delhi – 110025, India

79 Anson Road, #06–04/06, Singapore 079906

Cambridge University Press is part of the University of Cambridge.

It furthers the University's mission by disseminating knowledge in the pursuit of education, learning, and research at the highest international levels of excellence.

www.cambridge.org
Information on this title: www.cambridge.org/9781108461665
DOI: 10.1017/9781108562140

First published 2019

A catalogue record for this publication is available from the British Library.

ISBN 978-1-108-46166-5 Paperback
ISSN 2515-3986 (online)
ISSN 2515-3943 (print)

Gene–Culture Interactions

Toward an Explanatory Framework

Elements in Psychology and Culture

DOI: 10.1017/9781108562140
First published online: February 2019

Heewon Kwon and Joni Y. Sasaki
University of Hawaii at Manoa

Author for correspondence: Joni Y. Sasaki, yjoni@hawaii.edu

Abstract: Examining the interconnections between genes and culture is crucial for a more complete understanding of psychological processes. Genetic predispositions may predict different outcomes depending on one's cultural context, and culture may predict different outcomes depending on genetic predispositions – that is, genes and culture interact. Less is understood, however, about how genes and culture interact, or the psychological mechanisms through which gene–culture interactions occur. In this Element, Heewon Kwon and Joni Y. Sasaki review key findings and theories in gene–culture interaction research. Next, they discuss current issues and future directions in gene–culture research that may illuminate the path toward an explanatory framework.

Keywords: behavior genetics, culture

ISBNs: 9781108461665 (PB), 9781108562140 (OC)
ISSNs: 2515-3986 (online), 2515-3943 (print)

Contents

1 Introduction

What underlies or makes up the human mind has always been central to the nature–nurture debate. Despite historical philosophical arguments insisting that humans are substantially nature-determined (Plato and Hobbes) or, conversely, that humans are largely socially determined (Aristotle and Locke), today there is scientific consensus that both nature and nurture contribute to shaping the mind. The way in which nature and nurture work together, however, has yet to be settled, and integrative frameworks have emerged to address this gap in knowledge. This requires a broader perspective that includes both genes and culture, combining two seemingly disparate fields of research.

The study of individuals in connection to the cultural environment and to biology, separately, is not new. On the one hand, cultural psychology examines the impact of culturally shared social and environmental factors on the mind and behaviors (Markus & Kitayama, 1991; Segall, Lonner, & Berry, 1998; Shweder, 1991; Triandis, 2001; see also Kitayama & Cohen, 2010). As social beings, people are influenced by external factors – including diverse physical environments, social interactions, structures, institutions, values, and beliefs (Kim & Markus, 1999; Markus & Kitayama, 1991; Miyamoto, Nisbett, & Masuda, 2006) – the meaning of which is shared in a culture (Bruner, 1990). These factors jointly make up a culture and, in turn, can be considered the core of "nurture." Cultural psychology has historically studied these nurture-focused explanations for differences in actions, traits, and thinking across cultures, drawing a clear link between nurture and psychological processes. On the other hand, biology has aimed to understand human behavior as well, but by focusing on the physical mechanisms that connect humans to, and also distinguish us from, other organisms. The field experienced a rather rapid leap with the completion of the Human Genome Project in 2003. By uncovering the sequences of DNA and unfolding processes that lead to phenotype expressions (Meaney, 2017), combined with various neural and physiological processes that predict human behavior (Eccles, 1964; Morrell, 1961), the fields of biology and neuroscience have enriched scientific understandings of how nature shapes individuals. Although through different routes, both cultural psychology and biology have aimed to understand why humans think and behave the way they do.

Yet despite great progress in understanding human behavior within each perspective, it is possible that unexplained variance considered "noise" in one field could be explained by looking to the other field. Therefore, with two distinct pathways illuminating the underlying mechanisms of the human mind and behavior, it is perhaps a logical next step to understand how these paths may cross. Studying how cultural and biological factors interact may further our understanding of humans beyond what is possible in each field separately. Multidisciplinary work presents exciting new directions, but at the same time, it also introduces challenges that arise from combining different research methods and integrating disparate theoretical frameworks. Nonetheless, overcoming these challenges will ultimately enable us to understand the human mind to a fuller extent.

In this Element, we aim to provide a more nuanced understanding of human thought and behavior by using an integrated perspective of genes and culture. To do so, we first provide a review of gene–culture interaction research, covering key theories and empirical evidence that characterize this new area. Second, we discuss current issues in gene–culture interaction research, describing unique challenges that arise from integrating across fields. Finally, we conclude by highlighting future research directions, or opportunities for moving this new area forward.

2 Gene–Culture Interaction Review

This section reviews recent research within the framework of gene–culture interactions, including earlier frameworks and theories that led to its current form. First, we discuss preceding frameworks, such as the gene–environment interaction and gene–culture coevolutionary theory, and how the gene–culture interaction framework is related but also distinct. Then, we present empirical evidence demonstrating how cultural influences on various psychological processes, including cognitive processes, socioemotional behaviors, and well-being, can be moderated by genetic factors. After reviewing empirical work, we discuss key theories that lay an explanatory groundwork for gene–culture studies and provide new predictions for future research.

2.1 Overview of Frameworks

2.1.1 Gene–Environment Interaction (G x E) Framework

Contrary to the lay belief that genes wholly decide phenotypes, evidence from various fields, including biology, development, and cultural neuroscience, shows that genes do not solely determine characteristics. The environment can substantially influence genetic expression, with some genes never being expressed throughout an entire lifetime due to certain environmental conditions (Meaney, 2017; Rutherford, 2000). Given that both the environment and genes contribute to various phenotypic expressions or psychological outcomes, the gene–environment interaction (G x E) framework offers a useful and integrated perspective. More specifically, the G x E framework shifted the belief that a map of genes would directly link to behavioral and clinical outcomes to the understanding that the environment interacts at various levels of DNA expression (Meyer-Lindenberg & Weinberger, 2006), and thus the importance of studying both genes and environments as well as their interactions has become apparent.

Caspi and colleagues (2002, 2003) set a milestone for the gene–environment interaction framework, which triggered an array of subsequent studies revealing that, even if exposed to similar adverse experiences or environments, only individuals with certain genes were more likely to develop antisocial behaviors or depression. For instance, those with the homozygous short allele of serotonin transporter polymorphism (5-HTTLPR) were much more likely to experience depression when they went through a greater number of stressful events, while those with the long allele showed a much weaker or no association between the number of stressful events and depression (Caspi et al., 2003). This line of research showed how genes and environment can jointly shape psychological outcomes. In other words, people with certain genotypes may be predisposed to react more strongly to environmental factors than people with other genotypes, and at the same time, people with the same genotype might react differently when exposed to different environmental factors.

As was the case in some of Caspi's research (2002), many G x E studies considered early childhood experiences related to parenting style as a prominent environmental factor. One reason for this focus on parenting might be the abundant research on child temperament and parenting style interactions in developmental psychology (Rothbart, Posner, & Hershey, 2006). Past research suggests that children with difficult temperament show more internalizing or externalizing behaviors when they experience negative parenting or caregiving (Blackson, Tarter, Martin, & Moss, 1994; Bradley & Corwyn, 2008; Rothbart & Ahadi, 1994), while those who receive positive and sensitive parental care exhibit higher social competence (Pluess & Belsky, 2009) and social skills (Pluess & Belsky, 2010; Stright, Gallagher, & Kelley, 2008) in later childhood or adolescence. Based on this previous research, more recent studies focused on the genotype of the children instead of their temperament (Stein, Schork, & Gelernter, 2008), but parenting style remained as one of the most studied environmental factors. The importance of parenting is also supported by other genetic studies. For example, rodent maternal behaviors, such as licking and grooming, are known to influence the DNA methylation process in the early life of offspring (Weaver et al., 2004). For humans, the perception of parental rejection was shown to be associated with differences in DNA methylation patterns (Naumova et al., 2016).

While the environment may influence how genes are transcribed (DNA to RNA) or translated (RNA to proteins), including the unfolding process of DNA to phenotypic variations such as histone modification and DNA methylation (Meaney, 2017), the detailed process of transcription or translation is beyond the scope of this Element. Nonetheless, it is important to note that not all genotypes are directly expressed to phenotypes, and the influence of the environment can work at many levels. Reflecting the bulk of existing G x E studies in the current literature, most of the research discussed in this Element will involve single nucleotide polymorphisms (SNPs) and repeat polymorphisms, common types of DNA sequence variations that occur naturally in populations, and how they interact with different environmental factors.

2.1.2 Gene–Culture Interaction (G x C) Framework

Although much research based on the G x E framework has focused on parenting style and adverse home life as part of the early childhood environment, the "environment" is not limited to what a family provides in the home; environmental influences can also be seen later in life. The gene–culture interaction (G x C) framework builds upon and extends the G x E framework by incorporating culture as a relevant environmental factor across the lifespan. Culture is a set of values, institutions, and social structures that are loosely connected and shared among people (Kitayama, 2002) and thus is a comprehensive meaning system guiding thoughts and actions. In other words, cultural contexts embedded in the environment can influence every aspect of daily life, from experiences in childhood to those in adulthood. Culture, therefore, provides specific context-dependent challenges and motivations to people, and without understanding these particular characteristics in different cultures, researchers may only achieve partial knowledge of the way genes and the environment interact. The G x C framework lays a foundation for understanding how people with one genotype would be more responsive to certain cultural values or structures compared to others with a different genotype, and how those with the same genotype might exhibit different patterns of thoughts and behaviors as well as mental health outcomes depending on their culture.

2.1.3 Dual Inheritance Theory/Gene–Culture Coevolutionary Theory

Boyd and Richerson (1985) proposed a foundational theory regarding the relation of genes and culture called dual inheritance theory, also known as gene–culture coevolutionary theory (Chiao & Blizinsky, 2010; Fincher & Thornhill, 2012). The theory proposed that cultures have coevolved by interacting with genetic evolution. In other words, cultural values and traits are adaptive, and this adaptation influences and is influenced by genetic selection (Boyd & Richerson, 1985). Therefore, according to this theory, certain genotypes can lead people to attend to or show specific reactions to the environment, thus steering cultural selection. Culture as a form of environment may also influence genetic selection, for instance, if a genotype prospers because it imparts culturally rewarded or culturally valued traits (Odling-Smee, Laland, & Feldman, 2003).

Dual inheritance theory gained support from numerous empirical studies showing how a specific feature of culture interacts with certain genes (Chiao & Blizinsky, 2010; Mrazek, Chiao, Blizinsky, Lun, & Gelfand, 2013). For instance, research on level of lactose tolerance across Europe showed a positive association between dependence on milk products and lactose-tolerant population (Beja-Pereira et al., 2003), suggesting a historical coevolutionary link between cultural practices in milk production and people's biological ability to digest milk efficiently in these regions. In other research, Chiao and Blizinsky (2010) showed that countries with higher historical pathogen prevalence tended to be more collectivistic. The authors proposed that this positive association might be explained by the high frequency of serotonin transporter polymorphism (5-HTTLPR) short allele carriers. Furthermore, the frequency of short allele carriers in the population is actually negatively correlated to the rate of anxiety and depression, despite these carriers showing a higher tendency to express depression and anxiety (Lesch et al., 1996). Fincher and colleagues (2008) suggested that collectivistic values might have a buffering effect against not only pathogens but also environmental stress, therefore leading to the high frequency of people with short alleles in collectivistic cultures (Chiao & Blizinsky, 2010).

One criticism of research on human evolution and its developmental processes is that some older perspectives lacked explanation beyond simply claiming that it was adaptive (Gould & Lewontin, 1979), when findings in this area could be better explained by incorporating cultural factors (Andersson et al., 2014; Bogin, Bragg, & Kuzawa, 2014). For example, human reproduction and caregiving practices are distinct from other primates in that allocare and resources are transferred among not only those who are genetically related but also to non-family members and those without a close genetic relationship (Bogin et al., 2014). The authors suggest that this unique practice is a product of human culture and genes, called biocultural reproduction. The products of gene–culture coevolution are not limited to reproduction and caregiving practices and may also extend to language and religion (Ferretti & Adornetti, 2014). In other words, various practices in our lives may result from the coevolution of genes and culture rather than solely one or the other.

Although both dual inheritance theory (gene–culture coevolutionary theory) and gene–culture interaction acknowledge the importance of genes, culture, and their interplay, gene–culture interaction framework differs from dual inheritance theory in that it focuses on how the interplay manifests in individuals' daily lives. While dual inheritance theory provides a broad framework of how cultural evolution and genetic evolution co-occur by focusing on a macrolevel of analysis, the G x C framework attempts to understand how genetic and sociocultural factors jointly shape psychological processes and behaviors at the micro- or individual level (Kim & Sasaki, 2014). In other words, dual inheritance theory aims to understand the distribution of certain genes within specific cultural groups while the G x C framework aims to explain various psychological tendencies and behaviors through the interaction between certain genes and cultures. The findings we discuss in this Element have relevance for broader processes of genes and culture, including gene–culture coevolutionary theory. However, we focus primarily on the combined effect of gene and culture in various psychological processes and behaviors at the level of the individual via the G x C framework.

2.2 Empirical Evidence of Gene–Culture Interactions

In this section, we discuss empirical evidence that supports the gene–culture interaction framework. Although not exhaustive of the research done in this area, we review notable studies in various psychological domains, from early cognitive processes to long-term mental health outcomes. Through these studies, we can see how genes and culture jointly affect psychological outcomes and the importance of considering their interactive effect rather than trying to partition the proportions of nature versus nurture.

2.2.1 Perception and Attention

The earlier steps of cognitive processes include the perception of, and selective attention to, stimuli in the environment. A good deal of research in cultural psychology has shown how culture can influence people's perception and attention. For example, Masuda and Nisbett (2001) showed that East Asians and North Americans differ in their locus of attention such that East Asians tend to focus more on background information, while North Americans tend to attend more to focal objects. Within each culture, individual differences represent natural variation between individuals (Na et al., 2010), and according to the G x C framework, at least some individual differences may be explained by certain genotypes that are more or less susceptible to cultural influence. Therefore, numerous studies prompted by the G x C framework started to address these individual variances within a culture by focusing on genes that should theoretically link to certain individual differences.

A gene–culture interaction study on perception was done by Ishii and colleagues (2014), examining how people recognize the disappearance of facial expressions. Past studies have shown that East Asians are more sensitive to the disappearance of others' smiles due to the interconnected nature of collectivistic cultures and attention to social approval, compared to North Americans, whose individualistic culture emphasizes self-approval and satisfaction more (Ishii, Miyamoto, Mayama, & Niedenthal, 2011). While this general tendency differs across cultures, the authors propose that the sensitivity to those stimuli might differ depending on serotonin transporter (5-HTT), more specifically, 5-HTT gene-linked polymorphic region (5-HTTLPR). 5-HTT is known to play an important role in serotonergic neurotransmission regulation, which is deeply involved in cognition and emotional states. There are two types of alleles – short (s) and long (l) – of 5-HTTLPR, and short allele carriers show reduced binding of 5-HTT to the brain (Heinz et al., 2000). Short allele carriers are also known to show heightened attention to fear-relevant stimuli, higher sensitivity to emotional stimuli, as well as greater susceptibility to environmental stimuli in general (Beevers, Wells, Ellis, & McGeary, 2009; Caspi et al., 2003; Osinsky et al., 2008). Combining the expected effects of culture and genetic predisposition, the researchers predicted that among Japanese, those with the short allele of 5-HTTLPR would be more sensitive to the disappearance of a smile compared to 5-HTTLPR long allele carriers due to a greater sensitivity to relationship-threatening cues. However, among North Americans, there would be little to no difference between the short allele group and long allele group since the disapproval of others is less of a threatening cue. The results were in line with their hypothesis, thus providing support for the gene–culture interaction in perception of facial expressions, a relatively early stage in cognitive processes.

Another study that taps into gene–culture interactions on cognition was done by Kim and her colleagues (2010b) on how locus of attention differs by culture and could be moderated by genotype. A well-documented phenomenon is that there tend to be cultural differences between Eastern and Western cultures in locus of attention, whether people pay more attention to focal or contextual information in the environment. Due to the tendency to adopt a holistic style of reasoning, East Asians are prone to attend to the entire field, including background information, while North Americans who typically adopt an analytic style of reasoning, are prone to attend to focal objects more than background information (Nisbett, Peng, Choi, & Norenzayan, 2001). In addition to this cultural difference, research on cognitive flexibility found that 5-HT activity level influences the ability to attend to relevant stimuli while ignoring irrelevant information (Schmitt et al., 2000). Therefore, taking into account the role of 5-HTR1A, an autoinhibitor of 5-HT release, Kim and her colleagues examined whether the effects of 5-HTR1A interact with culture on locus of attention. They speculated that people homozygous for the guanine (G) allele, compared to those with cytosine (C) alleles, of 5-HTR1A would adhere more to the culturally dominant attentional locus – Westerners attending more to focal objects and East Asians attending more to background information. Indeed, the researchers found a linear trend among European Americans in the degree of attending to non-focal information such that people homozygous for the G allele paid the least attention to contextual, background information and those homozygous for the C allele paid the most attention, such that those with the heterozygous genotype were in between them. On the other hand, Koreans showed the opposite trend such that those homozygous for the G allele paid the most attention to contextual, non-focal information, and those homozygous for the C allele paid the least. In sum, cognitive processes, including the perception of and attention to stimuli, show different patterns depending on the genotype and the culture of people. By incorporating two seemingly distant fields, we are stepping forward in understanding how and why people think differently or similarly when faced with the same stimulus or situation.

2.2.2 Self-processes

Going beyond cognitive processes, studies from various fields support the interaction effect of genes and culture on how people construe the self. It would not be an exaggeration to say that one of cultural psychology's main areas of study has been the difference in the concept of self between the Eastern and the Western world. Building on cross-national research by Hofstede (1984), Markus and Kitayama (1991) showed there are striking differences in how people from different cultures conceptualize the self as relatively more independent, or distinct from others, versus more interdependent, or connected to close others. As was the case with cognitive processes, researchers soon investigated how genetic factors could moderate these processes.

One of the most widely observed cultural differences is in self-construal (Markus & Kitayama, 1991), with many Western societies showing independent social orientations and Eastern societies, especially East Asian countries, showing stronger interdependent social orientations (Singelis, 1994). Despite these broad cultural differences, individuals can also show important variation within the same culture (Na et al., 2010). Kitayama and his colleagues (2014) examined whether these individual differences could be due to one of the hypothesized plasticity genes – the dopamine D4 receptor gene (DRD4). DRD4, which is a repeat number polymorphism rather than a SNP, plays a role in regulating the dopamine pathway, which is related to the reward-processing areas of the brain (Delgado, 2007; Dreher, Kohn, Kolachana, Weinberger, & Beramn, 2009). Although previously known as the risk-seeking gene, DRD4 is now more widely understood to be related to reward sensitivity in general (e.g., Stice, Yokum, Burger, Epstein, & Smolen, 2012). Variation in the DRD4 polymorphism may thus be associated with sensitivity to reward, which, in turn, could influence how much people adhere to cultural norms, where adherence is usually associated with social rewards. More specifically, Kitayama and colleagues (2014) hypothesized that those with the plasticity DRD4 genotype, with 2- or 7-repeat alleles (2R or 7R), would endorse the culture-dominant social orientation more compared to those with the non-plasticity DRD4 genotype, with 4-repeat alleles (4R). The results showed that among 2R or 7R DRD4 carriers, there was a significant difference in the extent of independence endorsement between European Americans and Asian Americans, but no such difference was found among the 4R DRD4 carriers. These findings suggest that cultural norms about how to construe the self may be more meaningful to people with certain genetic tendencies. Although a cultural way of being may be widespread in a particular place, individuals can vary in the extent to which they internalize it.

Self-processes are not just confined to the concept of self alone but can be extended to how the self is viewed in relation with others (Markus & Kitayama, 1991). Attachment style is one of the foundational processes through which we develop relations between the self and close others and may have interesting implications in gene–culture research. LeClair and colleagues (2016) uncovered individual differences in attachment style depending on culture and genotype. Past literature showed that East Asians, especially Japanese, tend to have higher attachment anxiety and avoidance, while Americans show more secure attachment styles (Ishii et al., 2011; Rothbaum, Weisz, Pott, Miyake, & Morelli, 2000). Previous research has also shown that people with certain genes, including the oxytocin receptor polymorphism (OXTR), can be more or less susceptible to certain environmental influences (Kim et al., 2010a; Luo et al., 2015). OXTR rs53576 consists of G and/or A alleles, therefore one can carry one of the three genotypes – GG, AG, or AA – with the homozygous G allele carriers known to be more susceptible to particular features of cultural environments (Kim et al., 2010a). Taking these past findings into account, LeClair and colleagues (2016) predicted that those with the G allele would tend to have a more culturally common attachment style, and indeed they found that G-allele Japanese showed more avoidant attachment styles, while G-allele Americans showed a more secure attachment style. Overall, this study demonstrated that those with more socially sensitive genotypes tended to have an attachment style that is more common in their culture. Self-processes, including the concept of self or social orientations and attachment styles, are the basis of how people view the world and form relationships. Therefore, understanding the factors that influence self-processes may further our knowledge of psychological processes with implications much beyond the self.

2.2.3 Socioemotional Behaviors

Cognitive processes are an important part of psychology, but the emotional processes linked to cognitions, as well as the actual behaviors that result from them, are also crucial for a more complete picture of the mind. Socioemotional behaviors, including empathy and emotion regulation strategies, take a unique place in the intersection of genes and culture. Past literature has shown cultural differences in emotion processes (Mesquita & Walker, 2003), patterns of emotional experience and expression (Cohen & Nisbett, 1994; Fischer, 1999), as well as dominant emotions (Butler, Lee, & Gross, 2007; Kitayama, Markus, & Matsumoto, 1995). Considering the tight relation between physiological processes and emotions (Cannon, 1927), it is easy to see how genes, in interaction with sociocultural factors, may influence these processes and behaviors.

Empathy is understanding others' emotions and sharing their emotional states, and therefore, it taps into how much people can "feel" others. Due to the central component of connectedness with others, empathy has been investigated in relation to interdependent self-construal. Indeed, studies have shown that there is a positive correlation between interdependence and empathy (Joireman, Needham, & Cummings, 2002), and priming self-construal modulates empathic neural responses to the suffering of others (Jiang, Varnum, Hou, & Han, 2014). From a biological perspective, empathy is known to be linked with oxytocin, with past studies showing that administration of oxytocin increases emotional empathy (Abu-Akel, Fischer-Shofty, Levkovitz, Decety, &

Shamay-Tsoory, 2014; Sheng, Liu, Zhou, Zhou, & Han, 2013) as well as compassion (Kosfeld, Heinrichs, Zak, Fischbacher, & Fehr, 2005; however, see also Bartz, Zaki, Bolger, & Ochsner, 2011; Miller, 2013; Walum, Waldman, & Young, 2016 for review on the possible moderators of the effects of oxytocin administration). Taking these lines of research into account, Luo and colleagues (2015) examined the moderating effect of OXTR rs53576 in the relation between interdependence and empathy. In line with this past research, Luo and colleagues found that G (vs. A) allele carriers in a Chinese sample showed a stronger positive relation between interdependent self-construal and trait empathy, as well as empathic neural response activities. This study was done within a single culture, demonstrating that individual differences in a specific cultural orientation can interact with genes to predict empathic responses.

In addition to some cultural differences in empathy (Luo et al., 2015), there are clear cultural differences in when and what emotion regulation strategies to use. Emotion regulation strategies are present in every society, but the frequency and emphasis vary across cultures (Matsumoto, Yoo, & Nakagawa, 2008). For example, emotion suppression, or active suppression of one's emotion, is encouraged in East Asian countries since maintaining harmony is greatly valued. However, in America, emotion suppression is discouraged, while candid expression of emotions is valued (Matsumoto, Takeuchi, Andayani, Kouznetsova, & Krupp, 1998; Matsumoto, Yoo, Hirayama, & Petrova, 2005). The difference between East Asians and Americans in their encouragement of emotion suppression was well documented in cultural psychology; meanwhile, the field of emotion found evidence supporting that OXTR rs53576 is related to socioemotional sensitivity. In particular, the homozygous G allele carriers show greater parental sensitivity and empathic accuracy (Bakermans-Kranenburg & van IJzendoorn, 2008; Rodrigues, Saslow, Garcia, John, & Keltner, 2009). Therefore, Kim and her colleagues (2010) predicted that since emotion suppression is normative in East Asia, Koreans with a genetic predisposition for socioemotional sensitivity (GG genotype) would suppress their emotions more. Americans with the same genetic predisposition, however, would suppress their emotions less since the norm in their culture is to express their emotions. The study results confirmed their prediction and additionally showed that Asian Americans showed similar tendencies with Americans, likely due to their experience in a shared cultural context with Americans.

Not only do people have different tendencies to suppress naturally occurring emotions, but they also differ in which strategy to use when they are in need of emotional support. The cultural norm of seeking emotional support shows stark differences between Asian and American cultures. When exposed to stressors, Asians are less likely to seek emotional support from others compared to Americans because Asians are more concerned with the possible negative relational consequences from the act of support seeking (Taylor et al., 2004). Considering the cultural difference in emotional support seeking and the role of OXTR rs53576 in socioemotional strategy choices, Kim and her colleagues (2010a) examined whether people differed in seeking emotional support from others when they encounter stressful situations. The researchers examined Americans and Koreans and tested whether they would differ in their emotional support seeking tendency depending on their OXTR genotype. They found that among highly distressed individuals, American G allele carriers (GG/GA) were much more likely to seek emotional support compared to homozygous A allele carriers. However, highly distressed Koreans did not show a difference in their seeking tendency depending on their genotype, although G allele carriers showed a somewhat lower tendency to seek support. On the other hand, this gene–culture interaction was not present among low-distress individuals. In sum, these studies show that emotional processes and socioemotional behaviors in response to environmental factors (such as stress) are shaped by both genetic and cultural factors. More importantly, the latter two studies reveal that the expression of these characteristics might not always be present but unfolds in specific situations, showing that detecting gene–culture interactions requires careful attention to the cultural and social context.

2.2.4 Moral Behaviors

Although thought processes and behaviors all depend on multiple neural systems and interactions among them, perhaps one of the most complex cognitive processes is moral judgment and behaviors. Scholars consider morality to involve both sociocognitive skills and emotion-related processes (Chudek & Henrich, 2011). Because moral standards are known to differ greatly across cultures (Haidt, Koller, & Dias, 1993), taking a cultural approach may help predict how different sociocognitive skills are used and when different emotions are elicited in connection to moral behaviors. Further complicating matters, behavioral genetics studies show that certain genes, such as OXTR or DRD4, are related to moral judgments, ethnocentrism, and prosocial behaviors (Bachner-Melman et al., 2005; Bakermans-Kranenburg & van IJzendoorn, 2011; Bernhard et al., 2016; De Dreu, Greer, Van Kleef, Shalvi, & Handgraaf, 2011), and thus the gene–culture framework may be useful for examining an array of moral behaviors.

A study by Sasaki and her colleagues (2011) examined a gene–culture interaction on prosocial behaviors, which can be defined as acts that benefit others and can be seen as acts of "goodness" that tap into the concept of morality (Baron, 1997; Cialdini, 1991; Staub, 1978). Moreover, while there are various moral standards across the world, most religions emphasize prosociality as a virtue (Batson, Floyd, Meyer, & Winner, 1999). Supporting this, past behavioral research showed that inducing implicit thoughts of God increased prosocial behaviors (Shariff & Norenzayan, 2007; White, Kelly, Shariff, & Norenzayan, 2018; for a meta-analysis see also Shariff, Willard, Andersen, & Norenzayan, 2016). In regard to the relation between genes and prosocial behaviors, gene studies revealed an association between DRD4 susceptibility variants and prosocial behaviors (Bakermans-Kranenburg & van IJzendoorn, 2011). Therefore, considering religion as a form of culture, Sasaki and her colleagues (2011) examined how the effect of religion-priming on prosocial behaviors can be influenced by people's DRD4 genotype. The researchers found that religious priming was effective in increasing how much people were willing to volunteer, but only among DRD4 2R or 7R allele carriers, who are known to be environmentally susceptible, while the priming effect was not found among those without 2R or 7R alleles. This research raises the interesting possibility that religion may encourage people to behave more "morally" in some cases, but only for people with certain genetic predispositions. It seems that people with different genotypes of DRD4 may be behaving prosocially for different reasons. For people with an environmentally susceptible genotype, they may volunteer because religion compels them to do so, but for people without an environmentally susceptible genotype, they may not need pressures from religion to volunteer.

Further evidence in support of the gene–culture interaction model in moral behaviors comes from a study investigating altruism within the dictator game (Jiang et al., 2015). Altruism, an act of benefiting others at a cost for the actor (Bykov, 2017), is another form of prosociality and has been a popular subject among both economists and psychologists (Feldman, Cavalli-Sforza, & Peck, 1985; Forsythe, Horowitz, Savin, & Sefton, 1994; Henrich et al., 2005). Altruistic behaviors have been extensively studied using dictator games where two players are randomly paired, and the "dictator" decides to divide a certain amount of money or "good" while the other remains passive to the decision. Therefore, Jiang and colleagues (2015) used the dictator game paradigm to measure altruism and examined how religious affiliation and the previously used DRD4 genotype are associated with altruism. People could make selfish, effective, or fair decisions in the game, and the researchers observed how much people actually gave to their recipient compared to the predicted giving rate. The researchers found an association between religious affiliation and fair behaviors among male DRD4 non-4R allele carriers. In particular, Christian males with the susceptible (non-4R) DRD4 genotype showed significantly less selfish and fairer choices compared to non-Christian males with the same genotype. Despite there not being many studies that specifically investigated the interactive role of gene and culture on moral behaviors, these studies lay a foundation for fruitful future research.

2.2.5 Health and Well-being

Past cultural research has shown sociocultural factors to affect the association between psychological experiences and well-being (Suh, 2002), and gene studies have shown the influence of various genes on well-being and mental health (Ogilvie et al., 1996; Panicker et al., 2009). More recent studies have shown how genetic factors and cultural values can jointly shape one's well-being. For example, Dressler and colleagues (2009) showed the moderating role of cultural consonance, the perceived congruency of one's family's values and the culture's values, on the association between a polymorphism of the serotonin 2A receptor (5HT2A – 1438 G/A) and depressive symptoms in Brazil. Specifically, the researchers found that among those with the homozygous A allele of the serotonin receptor, cultural consonance was associated with a decrease in depressive symptoms. On the other hand, G allele carriers showed a much weaker association between cultural consonance and depressive symptoms. While conducted in only one cultural context, the authors show how endorsement of cultural values can moderate the genetic influence on important outcomes such as well-being.

Other research (Sasaki et al., 2011) has examined well-being as an outcome and tested how genes, culture, and religion may play a role. Past research on religion focused on its relation with well-being and whether involvement in religion would lead to positive well-being or health outcomes (George, Larson, Koenig, & McCullough, 2000). Most research leaned toward the positive outcomes of religion (McCullough, Hoyt, Larson, Koenig, & Thoresen, 2000), yet the strength of this association can be potentially influenced by culture and genes. An earlier study by Sasaki and Kim (2011) showed that even the same religion can have different meanings depending on culture. In particular, they found that Christian churches emphasize the value of secondary control (i.e., accepting and adjusting to hardship) in the United

States, where personal agency is a prioritized value, while they more strongly emphasize social affiliation in Korea, where social relationships are emphasized. Combining the different meaning of religion in different cultures (Sasaki & Kim, 2011) with findings that OXTR is linked to social sensitivity (Bakermans-Kranenburg & van IJzendoorn, 2008), the researchers examined if there was a three-way interaction between OXTR, culture, and religiosity on well-being. They found that religiosity is more strongly associated with psychological well-being among Koreans, for whom the social affiliation aspect of religion is more emphasized, compared to Americans. Moreover, this two-way interaction emerged only among OXTR G allele carriers, who tend to be more socially sensitive than A allele carriers. Therefore, by demonstrating this three-way interaction, the research supported how well-being may be linked to religiosity, but that it strongly depends on the broader cultural norms that shape religious values as well as individual genetic predispositions to be sensitive to those values in the first place.

While some research has examined the potential influence of culture and genes on the positive outcomes of mental health, others have focused on negative outcomes such as depression and suicide rate. For example, in a follow-up study to their research on depression and cultural consonance, Dressler and colleagues (2016) examined another cultural factor, social economic status (SES). According to Cohen (2009), SES can also be a form of culture where people in the same social class share similar values and beliefs (see also Kraus, Piff, & Keltner, 2011; Snibbe & Markus, 2005). In their longitudinal study, Dressler and colleagues (2016) showed how SES, childhood adversity, and genes have interactive effects on depressive symptoms. They revealed that while those with the AA genotype of 5HT2A who had high childhood adversity showed 45 percent more depressive symptoms compared to those who had low childhood adversity, G allele carriers reported only 5 percent more symptoms. This interaction showed a slightly stronger tendency among those in low SES families, although the three-way interaction did not reach significance. While depressive symptoms can be seen as warning signs of mental health issues, suicide rate could be an indicator of extreme threats to mental health. In a large cross-national study, Schild and colleagues (2014) found that the suicide rate differed by ethnicity and 5-HTTLPR. More specifically, the S allele acted as a protective factor for Caucasians but a risk factor for non-Caucasian populations. Although the authors do not propose a direct explanation for why the S allele could act as a protective factor in one ethnicity but as a risk factor in another ethnicity, it is possible that due to cultural differences in the way people cope with stressors (Kim et al., 2008), those from mainstream North American cultures may be more likely to seek support in the face of difficulties, offering a protective factor, compared to people from other cultures.

Depressive symptoms and suicide rates are broad indicators of well-being and mental health in a population. However, specific health-relevant behaviors, such as (lower) alcohol dependence and smoking, can also be useful indicators of well-being. A study by Chartier and colleagues (2016) adds weight to the framework of gene–culture interactions on health by revealing the joint effects of enzyme genes and religious involvement on alcohol dependence. Past research showed strong evidence for the positive association between alcohol dehydrogenase (ADH) enzyme genes and alcohol consumption as well as dependence (Hurley & Edenberg, 2012). Alcohol consumption and dependence are also known to be influenced by various social factors, including the protective effects of religious service attendance against alcohol consumption (Borders, Curran, Mattox, & Booth, 2010; Edlund et al., 2010). Therefore, taking both genetic and sociocultural factors into account, Chartier and colleagues (2016) tested if there is an interaction between ADH and religious attendance on alcohol dependence. Considering that religious attendance is greatly related to the perception of drinking norms within this particular religion, the authors predicted that religious attendance and ADH would have joint effects on alcohol dependence. Their results revealed that all three ADH risk variants showed weaker associations with alcohol dependence and maximum drinks when they were in the context of high religious involvement. Similar with alcohol dependence, smoking is discouraged in various religions, therefore showing an inverse relation between religiosity and smoking (Gryczynski & Ward, 2011). Timberlake and colleagues (2006) found that religiosity moderated the genetic influences on smoking among twins. Specifically, those with higher self-reported religiosity were less likely to start smoking compared to their twin who reported lower religiosity. Taken together, these studies show that well-being, mental health and health-related behaviors are dependent upon the collective and interactive effects of genes and culture.

2.3 Review of Theories

Research that investigates how specific genes can moderate sociocultural effects on psychological tendencies and behaviors is just in its initial stage. Despite the fairly short history of the gene–culture interaction framework, the number of studies in this area has steadily increased, reflecting growing interest. Studies based on the G x E or G x C frameworks and also other work incorporating genes and culture suggest that the full portrait of how the human mind and behaviors work may be better understood by considering genes, culture, and their interactions. In order to consolidate these various findings, a number of theories have been put forth to illuminate systematic patterns of results within a coherent explanatory model. In this section, we discuss several of these models that aim to uncover why these interactive effects emerge between genes and culture. For example, are certain genes linked to "good" or "bad" behaviors? Or are there genes that are "flexible" to the environment, whether good or bad? From the diathesis-stress model that focuses on negative environmental factors to the differential susceptibility hypothesis and motivational setting hypothesis that focus on the full range of external influences, different models tap into different aspects of gene–culture interactions. We present several models that have been suggested in the field and discuss how each may aid the understanding of the way genes and culture interact.

2.3.1 Diathesis-stress Model

The diathesis-stress model stipulates that individuals with vulnerable genes are predisposed to develop psychiatric disorders when exposed to adverse environments (Caspi, 2002, 2003; Monroe & Simons, 1991; Zuckerman, 1999). In other words, individuals can be carriers of adversity-vulnerable genes, but in order to develop a psychiatric disorder, it is necessary for these individuals to also encounter adverse environments, such as stress-inducing incidents or relationships. On the other hand, those without these genetic predispositions may not develop a psychiatric disorder even if they are exposed to the same environmental stressors. Numerous clinical and developmental studies have supported this model. For example, Belsky, Hsieh, and Crnic (1998) showed that externalizing behaviors of children were predicted from the combination of parent rearing styles and child temperament. Specifically, even if the child has a difficult temperament, such as negative emotionality, this did not predict later externalizing behaviors except when negative parenting practices were endorsed. Furthermore, Cummings, El-Sheikh, Kouros, and Keller (2007) found that individuals with higher skin conductance levels, possibly a phenotypic characteristic of a vulnerable genotype, had a higher risk of being negatively influenced by parental depressive symptomatology. In sum, the backbone of the diathesis-stress model is that certain genes increase an individual's vulnerability to adverse environments, possibly developing into psychiatric symptoms or disorders.

The idea of genetic vulnerability to negative environments opened up our understanding of how genes can interact with negative aspects of the environment and raised a number of questions relevant to cultural psychology. First, this research suggested that if certain genotypes show a sensitivity to negative home environments, it is possible that environments shaped by cultural norms may be similarly influenced. Second, given research that people in different cultures have varied ways of perceiving and coping with negative stressors in the environment (Kim et al., 2008), it is possible that some of the gene–environment interactions found under the diathesis-stress model are relevant in some cultures but not others.

2.3.2 Differential Susceptibility Hypothesis

Broadening the idea of stressor susceptibility, Belsky and colleagues (2007) proposed the differential susceptibility hypothesis, which suggests that individuals vary in susceptibility to the environment, whether it be positive or negative. More specifically, they insist that the same "risk" genes that develop into psychiatric disorders when the environment is negative can be expressed in the most beneficial way when the environment is positive (Belsky & Pluess, 2009; Ellis, Boyce, Belsky, Bakermans-Kranenburg & van IJzendoorn, 2011). Thus, genotypes are not inherently bad or good, but can be more or less sensitive to the surrounding environment, making them "plastic," not "vulnerable." While studies within the diathesis-stress model were restricted to negative experiences, the differential susceptibility hypothesis broadened the extent of potential influence to positive experiences. For instance, one study found that parents with DRD4 7-repeat genotype were less responsive to their toddlers when they had more than average daily hassles but were most responsive when the amount of daily hassles was low (van IJzendoorn, Bakermans-Kranenburg, & Mesman, 2008). In another study, adults carrying the T allele of serotonin 2A receptor showed the highest harm avoidance tendencies, having anticipatory anxiety toward threat or danger (Cloninger, Svrakic, & Przybeck, 1998), if they grew up in low socioeconomic status families, but the same genotype carriers were low on harm avoidance if they grew up in high socioeconomic status families (Jokela et al., 2007). Both studies show that depending on the environment, the same gene can be expressed in completely different ways. Interestingly, "plasticity" genes can lead to not only the worst but also the best outcomes. The differential susceptibility hypothesis moved away from the disproportionate focus on negative environments and outcomes to those that could be both good and bad, spurring new research on different types of environments, including cultural contexts. Yet the differential susceptibility hypothesis still raised the question of whether cultural contexts could be categorized as "good" or "bad" at all, opening the door to new frameworks that may more accurately capture the nature of environmental stimuli as they interact with genes.

2.3.3 Motivational Setting Hypothesis

So far, we briefly described different theories of how genes interact with different types of environments. All three theories focus on the valence of the environment and how people react differently depending on their genotype. However, another theory has been proposed, which focuses on the underlying reasons why people may be more or less responsive to environmental factors. The motivational setting hypothesis suggests that genetic variation might influence how motivated people are toward specific goals (Kim, Nasiri, & Sasaki, 2017). In other words, people with specific genotypes might be more motivated to achieve goals within related psychological domains such as reward, sociality, or anxiety compared to those with different genotypes. Therefore, regardless of the valence of the environment, people might have their own "default" strategies, or motivational settings, orienting them to specific goals depending on their genetic predispositions, but then they may switch strategies according to changes in the environment. For example, some people might be more motivated to gain rewards and have a default strategy to take high risks for short-term rewards. It is possible that when these individuals encounter a stable, resource-rich environment, they might switch their default high risk-taking strategy to a low-risk one since they can achieve rewards in the long-term without risking the uncertain negative consequences of high-risk strategies.

As an example, some research on DRD4 and prosociality shows that people with the 2R or 7R allele (vs. 4R) of DRD4 may seem more "antisocial," donating less to charity (Bakermans-Kranenburg & van IJzendoorn, 2011), showing more externalizing behavior (Bakermans-Kranenburg et al., 2008), and scoring lower on self-reported altruism (Bachner-Melman et al., 2005) and preference for fairness (Zhong et al., 2010). Yet people with these same "antisocial" genotypes actually seem to be the most prosocial when they experience supportive environments, such as secure attachment (Bakermans-Kranenburg & van IJzendoorn, 2011), maternal sensitivity (Bakermans-Kranenburg & van IJzendoorn, 2006), and maternal positivity (Knafo, Israel, & Ebstein, 2011). Knafo and colleagues (2011) found that even when maternal positivity was moderate, there was a significant difference between children with and without the 7R allele of DRD4, with 7R carriers being more prosocial than non-7R carriers. The inclusion of a moderate-level positivity group in this study raises a number of important issues in this area. First, "moderate" environments do not fit conceptually into previous theories that characterize environments as either good or bad. Other concepts, such as culture (Kim et al., 2010b) and religion (Sasaki et al., 2011), cannot be clearly categorized as wholly harmful or beneficial. Second, even if previous theories did somehow incorporate moderate or neutral environments, it is still unclear *why* people are responding in these ways to different environments. The advantage of the motivational setting hypothesis is that it offers an explanation, at the level of motivation, for why particular environments might be especially attention-grabbing and also evoke behavioral responses for certain people. For the Knafo et al. (2011) findings, it is possible that 7 R carriers were motivated to gain (in this case, social) rewards, and thus even a moderate level of maternal positivity was enough to encourage prosocial behavior for 7 R carriers compared to non-7 R carrier children, who were less motivated to gain social rewards. Further evidence and a deeper understanding of the psychological processes involved is needed; however, the motivational setting theory has the potential to expand the scope of the gene–environment interaction framework by pushing researchers to investigate why these interactions occur.

3 Current Issues in Gene–Culture Research

As science becomes increasingly interdisciplinary, unique opportunities and challenges arise. Working across fields can force scientists to listen to new voices, read different scientific "languages," and think critically about ideas that are radically new to them. This scientific cross-talk can be difficult but ultimately enables scientists to rethink some of their earlier assumptions and reimagine the implications of their work. For instance, interdisciplinary research often highlights the need for clearer definitions of terms or provides a novel solution to an age-old question. In this section, we discuss how integrating gene–environment interaction research with cultural psychology has raised unique questions about underlying assumptions of this work and also opens new possibilities for future research. We cover a number of current theoretical and methodological issues in gene–culture research, including: (1) the meaning of the "environment" in G x E, (2) problems with studying culture as environment, (3) dispelling assumptions of genetic determinism, and (4) the need for causal explanations. In so doing, we highlight future directions for new investigations in this burgeoning field.

3.1 Meaning of the "Environment" in G x E

One of the core assumptions of different G x E theories is that genetic susceptibilities and aspects of the environment interact in some way to produce differences in behavior. Yet a basic issue that remains unresolved in this area is that the meaning of the "environment" in gene–environment interactions is unclear. In the most literal sense, the environment could be the physical surroundings of people such as altitude of the place or the abundance of mountains. However, going beyond physical surroundings, social features of the environment, including political structures, interaction with peers, and parenting style, are inseparable parts of human life. Importantly, how people derive meaning from their physical and social world makes up a major part of the environment. What people perceive as important or pay close attention to in their surroundings may vary in crucial ways depending on aspects of the individual but also the broader culture (Leung & Cohen, 2011; Sasaki & Kim, 2017). The role of culture, providing social guidelines, values, and norms to the people within it, can be seen as a result of people's need for meaning and reflects the importance of meaning in humans. Therefore, gene–culture interactions highlight the need for meaning in G x E more broadly, and defining the aspects of the world that count as the environment (versus genes, for instance) may come with certain challenges.

A factor that potentially muddies the concept of the "environment" is other people or one's relationship with others. Past research has examined parenting and attachment as the environment in G x E (Rothbart et al., 2006), which is sensible from a social psychological perspective given that close others make up such a central part of our social world. Yet considering others as an environmental factor or an external force in G x E research complicates the issue because other people have their own genetic and environmental influences on their behaviors, making genetic (and antecedent G x E) effects latent in the environment. This issue is particularly relevant for parenting or family studies in which the "environment" includes genetically related others because each family member possesses their own genetic predispositions and subjective "environments" that add potential complexities to G x E models.

Whereas parenting styles and family atmosphere have been considered as major environmental factors, relationships without direct kinship are less considered as environmental or cultural factors. Nonetheless, various close others including peers, classmates, friends, and colleagues make up a large part of our lives, and several studies have considered peers as an environmental factor. For example, Buil and colleagues (2015) showed that the DRD4 gene moderated the association between the social standing of a child among her peers (i.e., social preference) and later conduct problems and prosocial behaviors. Specifically, only those with the DRD4 7R allele showed the association between social preference and conduct problems. Although this study did not incorporate culture, it shows how peers as an environmental factor can interact with genes to influence behavior. If we can take the genetic distribution among those peers or friend groups into account, this could reveal another layer of how genes and culture influence various behaviors. Therefore, understanding others as an environmental factor may need to be systematically divided into different levels of effects, such as family, peers, or friends, and the general population.

Moreover, the distribution of certain genes in one's close circle or the general population might have a unique effect. For example, having a common genotype with one's relationship circle might be different from having a minority genotype within the person's relationships and the general population. This opens up the possibility to view past research results from a different perspective. Take the study by Schild and colleagues (2014) on suicide rate as an example. In their study, the authors concluded that the 5-HTTLPR S allele is a protective factor for Caucasian countries and a risk factor for non-Caucasian countries. While differences in cultural values could explain the link between the S allele and negative psychological outcomes, the frequency or distribution difference of 5-HTTLPR S allele carriers across ethnicities (Li & He, 2007) might be a contributing factor. Considering that S allele carriers are the minority among Caucasians while they make up the majority of non-Caucasians, the position as a genetic minority, although not visible, might also contribute to the difference in its valence.

Additionally, the influence of others can differ depending on cultural differences in construal of self. For example, since East Asians incorporate others in their self-construal and value of collectivism, the influence of others might be much stronger than Westerners who view the self as a separate, unique entity (Markus & Kitayama, 1991). Therefore, it could be possible that the different distribution of certain genotypes might have a stronger effect among East Asians compared to Westerners. In other words, there is a possibility that there could be cultures that foster people to be more susceptible to the "majority" effect. If this turns out to be true, it could prompt various research questions regarding what happens when a person moves across completely different cultures (i.e., immigration), which is becoming more and more common in recent years (Oishi, 2010; U.S. Census Bureau, 2017).

3.2 Problems with Studying Culture as Environment

Understanding the definition of culture from a cultural psychological perspective may help gene–environment researchers to reconsider even basic terms in their investigations. The power of studying culture as the environment in G x E is that culture overlays meaning in the environment. Culture can help clarify what aspects of the environment people perceive as supportive (Kim, Sherman, & Taylor, 2008), motivating (Heine et al., 2001), or worthy of attention (Nisbett et al., 2001), and why. Indeed, a cultural approach provides exciting new ways to examine gene–environment interactions, but it can also introduce potential problems because of the way culture is defined and deeper issues surrounding the codependence of culture and biology.

The definition of culture is very broad, and there are many forms of culture, including (but not limited to) race or ethnicity, religion, socioeconomic status, and region (Cohen, 2009). Yet, in practice, most investigations in cultural psychology examine culture by comparing different ethnicities, and most commonly, people of (typically Western) European versus East Asian descent. This practice is also reflected in research on gene–culture interactions, which has often included people of different ethnicities as "culture" while examining individual variation in a gene (e.g., Ishii et al., 2014; Kim et al., 2010a, 2010b; Kitayama et al., 2014). A unique issue that arises from studying ethnicity as culture in this area of research is that "ethnicity," rather than solely representing one side of the gene x culture equation (i.e., culture), may actually lie at the intersection of genes and culture.

Ethnicity often refers to a group with shared ancestral history, including geographical region, language, and practices.[1] While there is no clear one-to-one mapping of genes to ethnic background, there are similar allele frequencies in populations that share historical geographical region (Tishkoff & Kidd, 2004). This means that using ethnicity as a proxy for culture introduces a potential confound in gene–culture studies: people of the same ethnicity may share not only cultural but also some biological factors. Including participants of East Asian ethnic backgrounds in a G x C study, for instance, may assume that people with this background share values or practices from the learned environment, but in addition, this group likely has a shared ancestry that traces back to a particular geographic region. Ethnicity thus may not be the clearest representation of cultural, as opposed to biological, factors in G x C studies.

One way to address this issue is to utilize the triangulation method, which involves adding a third cultural group (e.g., Asian Americans) to the typical

---

[1] Although lay understandings of "ethnicity" or "race" tend to group people into discrete categories, it is important to note that ethnic variation, from a biological perspective, is more continuous than categorical (Tishkoff & Kidd, 2004). It may be more useful to think of ethnicity as a cluster of people with largely shared but flexible characteristics rather than a group with rigid boundaries.

two-cultural-group design (e.g., East Asians vs. European Americans), in order to eliminate shared biology as a potential confound. For instance, Kim and colleagues (2010a) compared Koreans to Americans, and the American group was largely composed of European Americans but also included a sample of Korean Americans (i.e., who were ethnically Korean but were born and raised in the United States). The key results of their study showed that the gene–culture interaction held when comparing Koreans to Americans as the "culture" variable. Supplementary analyses showed that this same G x C interaction was significant when comparing only Korean Americans to Koreans, but it was not significant when comparing Korean Americans to European Americans. The Korean American group in this study was important for triangulating comparisons with both Koreans and European Americans. The analysis showing that Korean Americans were different from Koreans, but not from European Americans, supported the argument that the G x C interaction emerged due to a cultural, rather than biological, difference between the groups.

Another way to address this confound issue is to utilize experiments that manipulate culture or the environment. In a study that conceptualized religion as a form of culture, the salience of religion was manipulated to isolate potential effects of religious concepts on prosocial behavior (Sasaki et al., 2013). Results showed that religious salience increased prosocial behavior for people with certain variants of DRD4 (i.e., those with 2- or 7-repeat alleles), but this same effect did not occur for people with other DRD4 variants (i.e., non-2- or 7-repeat alleles). Future investigations could utilize cultural priming (Gardner, Gabriel, & Lee, 1999; Oyserman & Lee, 2008) or frame switching methods (Hong, Morris, Chiu, & Benet-Martinez, 2000) with participants of the same ethnic background in order to manipulate specific aspects of culture, independent of genes.

Methodological issues aside, there are perhaps deeper theoretical issues that arise from studying culture in G x C research. One issue to highlight is the codependent nature of genes and culture. The ways in which genes and culture overlap and influence each other, as in the concept of ethnicity, are highly complex and counterintuitive. There is a commonly held assumption, for instance, that genes simply represent "nature," and culture represents "nurture" and that, therefore, they are categorical and non-overlapping. This assumption may come, at least in part, from definitions of culture itself. Inherent in many definitions of culture is that it includes content in the world that is learned and created, or put simply, culture is the "man-made part of the environment" (Herskovitz, 1948, 1955, p. 305). This definition might at times be taken to mean that culture is entirely separate from biology. Culture, it may be assumed, is not part of the physical processes in humans or biological beings. Culture is in the values that we learn from our elders or the traditions we share during holidays. It is in the books we write and the songs we sing. In other words, culture is learned and made by humans. It is not nature, but nurture.

Although this nature–nurture dichotomy has long been explicitly rejected in scientific fields, its underlying assumptions remain in the ways we continue to talk about and study genes and culture. Even though researchers consider genes and culture as separate factors in G x C investigations, in reality, genes and culture are not completely independent, and furthermore, they can influence each other in complex ways over time.

As discussed earlier in this paper, theories in gene–culture coevolution (Chiao & Blizinsky, 2010; Feldman & Laland, 1996), or dual inheritance theory (Boyd & Richerson, 1985), suggest that genes can influence culture due to genetic predispositions to manipulate the cultural environment in particular ways, and culture can also influence genes because cultural practices may introduce environmental pressures that affect genetic selection in that group. Gene–culture coevolution theory is complementary, rather than an alternative, to the gene–culture interaction framework because they operate at different levels of analysis and across different timelines. Whereas the G x C framework allows predictions for present-day psychological processes at the micro level, gene–culture coevolution theory is meant to offer more distal explanations of macroevolutionary processes across longer periods of time in history. The interaction of culture and the genome over time has given rise to human minds that closely track norms governing behavior, explaining why humans are so (biologically) adept at adapting to new environments and learning from other people (Chudek & Henrich, 2011). Importantly, gene–culture coevolution theory has, at its core, a deeper assumption about the mutual influence of genes and culture on each other. Genes and culture change alongside, and because of, each other (Creanza & Feldman, 2016). Treating them as completely separate factors thus makes certain G x C findings difficult to interpret.

The issue of codependence of genes and culture applies more broadly to other types of gene–environment studies as well, as findings of genotype–environment covariance have shown that the more heritable a trait, the more culture dependent it is (Kan, Wicherts, Dolan, & van der Maas, 2013). In their research on genes, culture, and intelligence, Kan and colleagues (2013) found that performance on tests that were more culture-dependent showed greater heritability differences than on tests that were less culture-dependent. As an explanation, they argue that people with proclivities toward greater cognitive abilities tend to be surrounded by cognitively demanding environments, which tend to emphasize culture-dependent knowledge. This finding further highlights the potential problems with the nature–nurture dichotomy: if nature and nurture are correlated, it becomes difficult to separate them and assume they exert independent effects on traits or behaviors. The non-independence of genes and culture, and the way they mutually influence each other over time, are important issues to consider as researchers move forward in G x C investigations.

3.3 Dispelling Assumptions of Genetic Determinism

Cultural and genetic factors influence each other, as in gene–culture coevolution (Feldman & Laland, 1996), and they interact to lead to differences in behavior (Kim & Sasaki, 2014). Yet although genes and culture may not be independent, they are also not reducible to each other. Especially in light of research that gene–culture interactions have consequences for morality and health (Sasaki et al., 2011, 2013), it is crucial to dispel assumptions of genetic determinism and to highlight the point that culture and genes are not reducible to each other.

Genetic determinism – a specific form of biological determinism or reductionism – is the idea that explanations for people's thoughts and behaviors are ultimately based on genes or biology rather than external influences such as their environment. It is related to the psychological concept of genetic essentialism, or the tendency to view genetically based traits as determined and therefore unchangeable (Dar-Nimrod, 2012; see Dar-Nimrod & Heine, 2011 for review). The problem with genetic determinism and essentialism is that they are not accurate ways of understanding genetic influence, and furthermore, they can negatively impact motivational behaviors with real-world consequences, including math performance (Dar-Nimrod & Heine, 2006) and healthy eating choices (Dar-Nimrod & Heine, 2011). Thus, there are both theoretical and practical reasons to dispel the assumption that genes determine behavior.

Gene–culture coevolution theory suggests not only that genes can influence culture, but also that culture can influence genes via environmental pressures that impact on genetic selection, and yet there are a number of reasons, based on this theory, for why genes and culture are not reducible to each other. First, cultural change can occur much faster than genetic changes in a population, allowing humans to adapt quickly and flexibly to environmental factors without necessarily imposing long-term changes in the genome (Feldman & Laland, 1996). Humans and other social animals are able to learn from others, not just vertically (from generation to generation), but also horizontally (within a single generation), making it possible to enact change in a population via cultural transmission without the same time lag required in passing down one's genes. Because cultural change and genetic change are occurring at different rates, along with other important differences, it would be misguided to assume that genes and culture are ultimately reducible to each other.

Second, drawing on broader theorizing in cultural psychology, researchers have stated that cultural differences are not always reducible to individual differences (Na et al., 2010). They may just as well say that cultural differences are not always reducible to genetic differences, as genes are often assumed to be a source of individual differences. Data from Na and colleagues' (2010) large-scale study showed that across multiple measures of social orientation and cognitive style, there were predictable differences between cultural groups (in this case, between different socioeconomic classes) but no coherent individual-level relations. That is, working class people, as a *group*, were more interdependent and also more holistic than middle-class people overall, but *individuals* who were more interdependent were not necessarily the ones who were more holistic. Although these results may seem puzzling at first given evidence that social orientation and cognitive style are causally related (Kuhnen & Oyserman, 2002; see Grossmann & Jowhari, 2018 for pre-registered replication and Oyserman & Lee, 2008 for review and meta-analysis), the authors point out that the reasons for group differences in a construct are likely to be different from the reasons individuals might differ in that same construct (Na et al., 2010). Similarly, the reasons cultures differ in a construct are likely to be different from the reasons individuals differ at the level of genes.

In a particularly clarifying example of this point, the authors write that a colleague of theirs told them, "I propose a new construct which I'll label 'Asianness,' which is based on a tolerance for dense crowds, skill using chopsticks, having dark hair color, and a preference for soy products. I imagine that if I investigated this, I would find pronounced cultural differences between East Asia and North America on each of these individual measures. Is Asianness a cultural construct?" (Na et al., 2010, p. 6195). The authors highlight that this construct would be nonsensical, and a related point perhaps is that there may be no such thing as "culture absorbers," or individuals who tend to be high on every trait or behavior that is typical in a given culture. The nature of group processes is that individuals, together, combine in a group to become more than the sum of their parts. They begin to take on group characteristics and emotions that have consequence for their own identities and their interactions with others (Mackie & Smith, 2014; Mackie, Smith, & Ray, 2008), all in the name of the group. But although it is possible to characterize a group in a particular way, it may be uncommon that there are certain *individuals* in that group that are solely responsible for characterizing the group as a whole. Instead it may be the case that each individual may highly embody certain, but not all, traits or behaviors that characterize the group as a gestalt.

The idea that there are no culture absorbers is consistent with empirical evidence in G x C research showing that gene–culture interactions do not seem to occur across the board for all psychological outcomes. Rather, gene–culture interactions seem sensitive to the psychological relevance of the particular genes of interest. For instance, one study showed a gene–culture interaction on emotion regulation such that Koreans with the GG genotype of OXTR were more likely to suppress their emotions than those with the AA genotype; however, Americans showed the opposite pattern, with GG genotypes suppressing emotions less than AA genotypes (Kim et al., 2011). OXTR has been shown to be relevant to socioemotional behaviors, such as empathic accuracy (Rodrigues et al., 2009) and sensitive parenting behavior (Bakermans-Kranenberg & van IJzendoorn, 2008). Thus, it seems reasonable that this particular gene–culture interaction occurs on emotion regulation, but not necessarily on outcomes less related to socio-emotional sensitivity. Another gene–culture study demonstrated an interaction between culture and 5-HT1A, which is relevant to cognitive flexibility and attention, on analytic versus holistic locus of attention (Kim et al., 2010b). This study also showed the predicted gene–culture interaction, with people carrying the environmentally susceptible genotype showing the more culturally normative locus of attention tendency. Yet, theoretically, it seems less likely that people with certain genotypes of a particular gene – say, OXTR or 5-HT1A – should show the culturally normative tendency across many different psychological domains, such as emotion, attention, social orientation, motivation, and so on. Just as the same individuals do not seem to be upholding all cultural norms across psychological tendencies (Na et al., 2010), it is unlikely that any single genotype would be linked to culturally normative tendencies across the board. Cultural norms cannot be reduced to individual, or genetic, differences. To further complicate matters, because most traits and behaviors rely on complex interactions between genes and the environment, genetic determinism is an especially unlikely explanation for psychological outcomes.

3.4 The Need for Causal Explanations

The basic premise of G x E – that individuals may respond slightly differently even in the same situation – is one that resonates with many from an individual difference perspective. At the same time, from a social psychological perspective, it is known that an individual can be swayed by the power of the situation. G x E encapsulates both these ideas, demonstrating that they are complementary. However, a G x E statistical interaction on any particular outcome is not enough for a deeper understanding of the psychological processes driving the effect.

One of the main theoretical challenges in G x E research is that findings of G x E are statistical interactions, demonstrating *when* a particular effect occurs, but they do not offer causal explanations. In a statistical interaction, the effect of one factor is different depending on levels of another factor; the genetic effect is moderated by the environment, or vice versa, in gene–environment interactions. Yet *why* the interaction occurs, and *how*, are separate questions.

This issue may be clarified with an example. For many gene–culture (and by extension, G x E) interaction effects, there is a spreading interaction: for people with one genotype, there is an effect of culture, but for those with another genotype, there is little to no effect of culture. This interaction effect occurs, theoretically, because people with certain genotypes are more sensitive to environmental influence, while others are less susceptible. Among a number of different perspectives, the differential susceptibility hypothesis in particular emphasizes that some people may be more susceptible to environmental influences, "for better and for worse" – that is, whether their environments are beneficial or harmful (Belsky et al., 2007). In order to explain why there is an effect of culture or the environment for people with one genotype but not the other, there still needs to be a psychological explanation for why people are sensitive to certain environments in the first place.

Because the concept of the "environment" in G x E seems to include social and non-social surroundings of both positive and negative valence, influence from the "environment" could potentially range from the threat of bad weather, to the excitement of exotic travel, or approval from one's parent. Because of this incredible range of content, it is unclear from the perspective of personality psychology what the reason could be for a person to be more sensitive to such a variety of environments. For instance, people high on neuroticism may be susceptible to life stressors or threats because of emotional instability. People high on openness to experience may be especially drawn by environments that are novel because they crave stimulation. People high on agreeableness may be susceptible to influence from other people because they care about social approval. There are many personality traits that suggest a level of environmental susceptibility, but the specific type of environment may be relevant for drawing a connection to a particular personality trait. It does not seem consistent with current personality theory to posit that people with certain genotypes may be more sensitive across the board to, say, stress, novelty, and social approval. Instead it seems more likely that people with certain genotypes may be sensitive only to particular features of the environment.

There are many missing steps in the path from genes to behavior.[2] One possible next step for understanding why people with certain genetic tendencies are sensitive to particular features of the environment in the first place may be to use personality as a mediating variable in G x E interactions predicting psychological outcomes. Although there is unlikely to be a one-to-one mapping between genes and personality traits, certain traits with neurobiological relevance to the target gene(s) may be useful to consider as mediators because personality can help explain why people are motivated toward particular behaviors across seemingly disparate situations.

However, in addition, any link between personality and behavior can be moderated by the situation, as articulated in classic interactionist perspectives such as the person-by-situation approach (Mischel & Shoda, 1995). Because situations are shaped by the broader cultural context that provides meaning to them (Leung & Cohen, 2011), culture further moderates the situational influence on the personality-to-behavior link. If, as stated earlier, interactions are not necessarily explanations, then surely the three-way personality x situation x culture interaction that links genes to behavior is not a satisfying explanation for why people with certain genes interact with certain features of the environment to lead to different behaviors. It is perhaps unsatisfying because with these additional interactions comes the need for further explanatory mechanisms. What are the reasons people with certain personalities are influenced by particular cultural situations to behave one way or another? Here one explanation may be that people with certain personalities have specific motivations or goals they are trying to fulfill. They are sensitive to aspects of culturally shaped situations depending on their underlying motivations, and they behave in ways that ultimately aim to satisfy those motivations.

The motivational setting hypothesis may lay the groundwork for identifying which personality traits, or "motivational settings," provide useful explanations for G x E effects. Based on people's different motivational settings, they may be more likely to attend to certain information, or interpret the information in a particular way, and then act on their perceptions accordingly. In short, these motivations provide reasons for environmental influence and are specific to the content domain.

---

[2] For instance, there are neuroendocrine responses that lead up to and accompany behaviors, which can trigger epigenetic processes that affect gene expression, further complicating the pathways between genes and behavior.

For instance, based on research involving dopamine pathways, it appears that a relevant motivational setting for dopamine-related genes would be reward sensitivity. Research on the dopamine receptor D4 (D4R) shows that inefficient or absent D4Rs are linked to changes in the inhibitory dopaminergic signal (Oak, Oldenhof, & Van Tol, 2000) and dopamine synthesis (Rubinstein et al., 1997), which has consequences for excitability for rewards (Forbes et al., 2009) and motion or task performance when given reward stimuli (Rubenstein et al., 1997). Thus, one possible psychological explanation for these effects is that people with the susceptibility genotype of dopamine-related genes are more sensitive to the prospect of reward. Having the goal of attaining rewards motivates them to attend to reward-relevant information, interpret information as reward-relevant, and/or behave in a way that helps them achieve rewards.

As discussed earlier, it is also an open question as to where, psychologically, gene–culture interactions occur, and the answer to this question is likely complex. The mechanisms underlying these interactions may occur at the level of attention, perception, or interpretation of stimuli, and the precise mechanism may vary depending on the gene and behavior of interest. For instance, in research on the interaction between genes and an environmental manipulation (i.e., an implicit prime) of religious salience, people were more likely to behave prosocially after being primed with religion, but only among those who had the environmentally susceptible genotype of DRD4 (Sasaki et al., 2013). In this study, however, there was no evidence that people with different genotypes of DRD4 were differentially attentive to the prime itself. The study included an explicit measure of religiosity as a manipulation check, and people with susceptible and non-susceptible genotypes of DRD4 both reported higher religiosity after being primed with religion than not. Because there was no difference between genotypes in this basic influence of the prime, this suggests that DRD4 may not change the way people attend to or perceive various information. Regardless of genotype, people seemed to attend to the prime and subsequently perceived the prime as self-relevant given that the manipulation check was significant across participants overall and within each genotype. Yet when it came to the influence of the prime on a behavioral outcome – in this case, prosocial behavior – there was a significant difference depending on genotype. This finding suggests that people with different genotypes may be *interpreting* the prime differently in connection to the behavioral outcome, perhaps because they have different goals. People with environmentally susceptible genotypes may be more motivated to increase feelings of reward. Thus, the link between religion and prosocial behavior may be stronger for them because religion tends to emphasize that behaving prosocially toward others comes with a lack of punishment (Shariff & Norenzayan, 2007), or perhaps, the prospect of reward. However, people without environmentally susceptible genotypes may be less motivated to increase feelings of reward, so for them, the link between religion and prosocial behavior is not as strong. Overall these findings suggest that this gene–culture interaction may be explained at the level of interpretation of stimuli: there are differences in the way people with different genotypes interpret the information they have already attended to and perceived.

4 Future Directions

The research we highlight in this Element demonstrates the joint effects of culture and genes in various psychological domains. Under the broad assumptions of the nature–nurture dichotomy, researchers might have previously understood genetic and cultural factors separately in the way they shape the human mind and behaviors. Yet by taking both genetic and cultural factors into account, these gene–culture interaction studies provide us with a deeper and more comprehensive understanding of how our thoughts, self-concepts, behaviors and well-being are shaped. Systematic patterns of G x C results have emerged in some areas, leading to theoretical frameworks that can consolidate findings. Yet as a field in its early stage, G x C research still has numerous obstacles to overcome, presenting clear opportunities for future research.

Despite great progress in G x E and G x C research, one shortcoming is that the types of genes used in these studies are relatively limited. For example, most of the research we reviewed has examined OXTR, 5-HTTLPR, or DRD4. In addition to the limited number of genes studied, many of these genes were single nucleotide polymorphisms (SNPs), which might be an oversimplification of the genetic model (Halldorsdottir & Binder, 2017). For a more in-depth understanding, it is necessary to expand the types of genes studied. There have been some G x E studies that have targeted other genes that moderate stress response and regulate hypothalamic-pituitary-adrenal (HPA) such as FKBP5 (Zannas, Wiechmann, Gassen, & Binder, 2016), CRHR1 (Corticotropin-Releasing Hormone Receptor; Binder & Nemeroff, 2010), and COMT (Catechol-O-Mathyltransferase; Caspi, Moffitt, Caoonon, McClay, Murray, Harrington et al., 2005). However, future studies need to consider other genes and their interactive effects with culture.

In addition to the need for a wider range of genes to be studied, consideration of gene x gene interactions within the G x C framework is needed as well. Past studies mostly focused on only one gene, but multiple genes can interact with each other, requiring a more nuanced approach in selecting which genes to investigate. One exciting new approach is the polygenic risk score (PRS) analysis, which incorporates the combined effects of many common genetic variants, thus representing the additive effect of multiple SNPs (Halldorsdottir & Binder, 2017; Rutter, Moffitt, & Caspi, 2006). Several studies have already shown the advantages of PRS: larger cumulative effect sizes and predictive power (Bulik-Sullivan et al., 2015; LeClair, Janusonis, & Kim, 2014; Mullins et al., 2016). Therefore, incorporating various genes and ground-breaking methods will be necessary for a more complete understanding of psychological tendencies and behaviors.

Many of the most basic questions posed in science are the most intriguing: What makes people so similar from place to place and yet, at the same time, undeniably unique? How are we so compelled to learn things from our environment or culture while also being led by our own biological "instincts"? Answers to questions like these may come from thinking beyond a single framework or discipline. Integrative frameworks, like that of gene–culture interactions, and interdisciplinary fields, such as cultural neuroscience, may evoke some of the greatest challenges but also unearth some of the most gratifying rewards in our search for nuance and explanation.

References

Abu-Akel, A., Fischer-Shofty, M., Levkovitz, Y., Decety, J., & Shamay-Tsoory, S. (2014). The role of oxytocin in empathy to the pain of conflictual out-group members among patients with schizophrenia. *Psychological Medicine, 44* (16), 3523–3532.

Andersson, C., Törnberg, A., Törnberg, P., Davidson, I., Hovers, E., Belfer-Cohen, A., . . . & Read, D. W. (2014). An evolutionary developmental approach to cultural evolution. *Current Anthropology, 55* (2), 154–174.

Bachner-Melman, R., Gritsenko, I., Nemanov, L., Zohar, A. H., Dina, C., & Ebstein, R. P. (2005). Dopaminergic polymorphisms associated with self-report measures of human altruism: a fresh phenotype for the dopamine D4 receptor. *Molecular Psychiatry, 10*(4), 333.

Bakermans-Kranenburg, M. J., & Van IJzendoorn, M. H. (2006). Gene-environment interaction of the dopamine D4 receptor (DRD4) and observed maternal insensitivity predicting externalizing behavior in preschoolers. *Developmental Psychobiology: The Journal of the International Society for Developmental Psychobiology, 48*(5), 406–409.

(2008). Oxytocin receptor (OXTR) and serotonin transporter (5-HTT) genes associated with observed parenting. *Social Cognitive and Affective Neuroscience, 3*, 128–134.

(2011). Differential susceptibility to rearing environment depending on dopamine-related genes: New evidence and a meta-analysis. *Development and Psychopathology, 23*(1), 39–52.

Bakermans-Kranenburg, M. J., Van IJzendoorn, M. H., Pijlman, F. T., Mesman, J., & Juffer, F. (2008). Experimental evidence for differential susceptibility: dopamine D4 receptor polymorphism (DRD4 VNTR) moderates intervention effects on toddlers' externalizing behavior in a randomized controlled trial. *Developmental Psychology, 44*(1), 293.

Baron, J. (1997). The illusion of morality as self-interest: A reason to cooperate in social dilemmas. *Psychological Science, 8*(4), 330–335.

Bartz, J. A., Zaki, J., Bolger, N., & Ochsner, K. N. (2011). Social effects of oxytocin in humans: context and person matter. *Trends in Cognitive Sciences, 15*(7), 301–309.

Batson, C. D., Floyd, R. B., Meyer, J. M., & Winner, A. L. (1999). "And who is my neighbor?": Intrinsic religion as a source of universal compassion. *Journal for the Scientific Study of Religion*, 445–457.

Beevers, C. G., Wells, T. T., Ellis, A. J., & McGeary, J. E. (2009). Association of the serotonin transporter gene promoter region (5-HTTLPR) polymorphism with biased attention for emotional stimuli. *Journal of Abnormal Psychology, 118*(3), 670.

Beja-Pereira, A., Luikart, G., England, P. R., Bradley, D. G., Jann, O. C., Bertorelle, G., ... & Erhardt, G. (2003). Gene-culture coevolution between cattle milk protein genes and human lactase genes. *Nature Genetics, 35*(4), 311.

Belsky, J., Bakermans-Kranenburg, M. J., & van IJzendoorn, M. H. (2007). For better and for worse: Differential susceptibility to environmental influences. *Current Directions in Psychological Science, 16*(6), 300–304.

Belsky, J. A. Y., Hsieh, K. H., & Crnic, K. (1998). Mothering, fathering, and infant negativity as antecedents of boys' externalizing problems and inhibition at age 3 years: Differential susceptibility to rearing experience? *Development and Psychopathology, 10*(2), 301–319.

Belsky, J., & Pluess, M. (2009). Beyond diathesis stress: differential susceptibility to environmental influences. *Psychological Bulletin, 135*(6), 885.

Bernhard, R. M., Chaponis, J., Siburian, R., Gallagher, P., Ransohoff, K., Wikler, D., ... & Greene, J. D. (2016). Variation in the oxytocin receptor gene (OXTR) is associated with differences in moral judgment. *Social Cognitive and Affective Neuroscience, 11*(12), 1872–1881.

Binder, E. B., & Nemeroff, C. B. (2010). The CRF system, stress, depression and anxiety – insights from human genetic studies. *Molecular Psychiatry, 15*(6), 574.

Blackson, T. C., Tarter, R. E., Martin, C. S., & Moss, H. B. (1994). Temperament mediates the effects of family history of substance abuse on externalizing and internalizing child behavior. *American Journal on Addictions, 3*(1), 58–66.

Bogin, B., Bragg, J., & Kuzawa, C. (2014). Humans are not cooperative breeders but practice biocultural reproduction. *Annals of Human Biology, 41*(4), 368–380.

Borders, T. F., Curran, G. M., Mattox, R., & Booth, B. M. (2010). Religiousness among at-risk drinkers: Is it prospectively associated with the development or maintenance of an alcohol-use disorder? *Journal of Studies on Alcohol and Drugs, 71*(1), 136–142.

Boyd, R., Richerson, P. J. (1985). *Culture and the Evolutionary Process.* Chicago, IL: The University of Chicago Press.

Bradley, R. H., & Corwyn, R. F. (2008). Infant temperament, parenting, and externalizing behavior in first grade: A test of the differential susceptibility hypothesis. *Journal of Child Psychology and Psychiatry, 49*(2), 124–131.

Bruner, J. (1990). Culture and human development: A new look. *Human Development, 33*(6), 344–355.

Buil, J. M., Koot, H. M., Olthof, T., Nelson, K. A., & van Lier, P. A. (2015). DRD4 genotype and the developmental link of peer social preference with conduct problems and prosocial behavior across ages 9–12 years. *Journal of Youth and Adolescence, 44*(7), 1360–1378.

Bulik-Sullivan, B., Finucane, H. K., Anttila, V., Gusev, A., Day, F. R., Loh, P. R., ... & Daly, M. J. (2015). An atlas of genetic correlations across human diseases and traits. *Nature Genetics, 47*(11), 1236.

Butler, E. A., Lee, T. L., & Gross, J. J. (2007). Emotion regulation and culture: Are the social consequences of emotion suppression culture-specific? *Emotion, 7*(1), 30.

Bykov, A. (2017). Altruism: New perspectives of research on a classical theme in sociology of morality. *Current Sociology, 65*(6), 797–813.

Cannon, W. B. (1927). The James-Lange theory of emotions: A critical examination and an alternative theory. *The American Journal of Psychology, 39* (1/4), 106–124.

Caspi, A., McClay, J., Moffitt, T. E., Mill, J., Martin, J., Craig, I. W., ... & Poulton, R. (2002). Role of genotype in the cycle of violence in maltreated children. *Science, 297*(5582), 851–854.

Caspi, A., Moffitt, T. E., Cannon, M., McClay, J., Murray, R., Harrington, H., ... & Poulton, R. (2005). Moderation of the effect of adolescent-onset cannabis use on adult psychosis by a functional polymorphism in the catechol-O-methyltransferase gene: longitudinal evidence of a gene X environment interaction. *Biological Psychiatry, 57*(10), 1117–1127.

Caspi, A., Sugden, K., Moffitt, T. E., Taylor, A., Craig, I. W., Harrington, H., ... & Poulton, R. (2003). Influence of life stress on depression: moderation by a polymorphism in the 5-HTT gene. *Science, 301*(5631), 386–389.

Chartier, K. G., Dick, D. M., Almasy, L., Chan, G., Aliev, F., Schuckit, M. A., ... & Nurnberger Jr, J. (2016). Interactions between alcohol metabolism genes and religious involvement in association with maximum drinks and alcohol dependence symptoms. *Journal of Studies on Alcohol and Drugs, 77*(3), 393–404.

Chiao, J. Y., & Blizinsky, K. D. (2010). Culture–gene coevolution of individualism–collectivism and the serotonin transporter gene. *Proceedings of the Royal Society of London B: Biological Sciences, 277* (1681), 529–537.

Chudek, M., & Henrich, J. (2011). Culture–gene coevolution, norm-psychology and the emergence of human prosociality. *Trends in Cognitive Sciences, 15*(5), 218–226.

Cialdini, R. B. (1991). Altruism or egoism? That is (still) the question. *Psychological Inquiry, 2*(2), 124–126.

Cloninger, C. R., Svrakic, D. M., & Przybeck, T. R. (1998). A psychobiological model of temperament and character. *The Development of Psychiatry and Its Complexity*, 1–16.

Cohen, A. B. (2009). Many forms of culture. *American Psychologist, 64*, 194–204.

Cohen, D., & Nisbett, R. E. (1994). Self-protection and the culture of honor: Explaining southern violence. *Personality and Social Psychology Bulletin, 20*(5), 551–567.

Creanza, N., & Feldman, M. W. (2016). Worldwide genetic and cultural change in human evolution. *Current Opinion in Genetics and Development, 41*, 85–92.

Cummings, E. M., El-Sheikh, M., Kouros, C. D., & Keller, P. S. (2007). Children's skin conductance reactivity as a mechanism of risk in the context of parental depressive symptoms. *Journal of Child Psychology and Psychiatry, 48*(5), 436–445.

Dar-Nimrod, I. (2012). Post-genomics and genetic essentialism. *Behavioral and Brain Sciences, 35*, 362–363.

Dar-Nimrod, I., & Heine, S. J. (2006). Exposure to scientific theories affects women's math performance. *Science, 314*, 435.

(2011). Genetic essentialism: On the deceptive determinism of DNA. *Psychological Bulletin, 137*, 800–818.

De Dreu, C. K., Greer, L. L., Van Kleef, G. A., Shalvi, S., & Handgraaf, M. J. (2011). Oxytocin promotes human ethnocentrism. *Proceedings of the National Academy of Sciences, 108*(4), 1262–1266.

Delgado, M. R. (2007). Reward-related responses in the human striatum. *Annals of the New York Academy of Sciences, 1104*(1), 70–88.

Dreher, J. C., Kohn, P., Kolachana, B., Weinberger, D. R., & Berman, K. F. (2009). Variation in dopamine genes influences responsivity of the human reward system. *Proceedings of the National Academy of Sciences, 106*(2), 617–622.

Dressler, W. W., Balieiro, M. C., de Araújo, L. F., Silva, W. A., & dos Santos, J. E. (2016). Culture as a mediator of gene-environment interaction: Cultural consonance, childhood adversity, a 2A serotonin receptor polymorphism, and depression in urban Brazil. *Social Science and Medicine, 161*, 109–117.

Dressler, W. W., Balieiro, M. C., Ribeiro, R. P., & Santos, J. E. D. (2009). Cultural consonance, a 5HT2A receptor polymorphism, and depressive symptoms: A longitudinal study of gene × culture interaction in urban

Brazil. *American Journal of Human Biology: The Official Journal of the Human Biology Association, 21*(1), 91–97.

Eccles, J. C. (1964). Structural features of chemically transmitting synapses. In *The Physiology of Synapses* (pp. 11–26). Springer, Berlin, Heidelberg.

Edlund, M. J., Harris, K. M., Koenig, H. G., Han, X., Sullivan, G., Mattox, R., & Tang, L. (2010). Religiosity and decreased risk of substance use disorders: is the effect mediated by social support or mental health status? *Social Psychiatry and Psychiatric Epidemiology, 45*(8), 827–836.

Ellis, B. J., Boyce, W. T., Belsky, J., Bakermans-Kranenburg, M. J., & Van IJzendoorn, M. H. (2011). Differential susceptibility to the environment: An evolutionary–neurodevelopmental theory. *Development and Psychopathology, 23*(1), 7–28.

Feldman, M. W., Cavalli-Sforza, L. L., & Peck, J. R. (1985). Gene-culture coevolution: models for the evolution of altruism with cultural transmission. *Proceedings of the National Academy of Sciences, 82*(17), 5814–5818.

Feldman, M. W., & Laland, K. N. (1996). Gene–culture co-evolutionary theory. *Trends in Ecology and Evolution, 11*, 453–457.

Ferretti, F., & Adornetti, I. (2014). Biology, culture and coevolution: Religion and language as case studies. *Journal of Cognition and Culture, 14*(3–4), 305–330.

Fincher, C. L., & Thornhill, R. (2012). Parasite-stress promotes in-group assortative sociality: The cases of strong family ties and heightened religiosity. *Behavioral and Brain Sciences, 35*(2), 61–79.

Fincher, C. L., Thornhill, R., Murray, D. R., & Schaller, M. (2008). Pathogen prevalence predicts human cross-cultural variability in individualism/ collectivism. *Proceedings of the Royal Society of London B: Biological Sciences, 275*(1640), 1279–1285.

Fischer, A. H. (1999). The role of honour-related vs. individualistic values in conceptualising pride, shame, and anger: Spanish and Dutch cultural prototypes. *Cognition and Emotion, 13*(2), 149–179.

Forbes, E. E., Brown, S. M., Kimak, M., Ferrell, R. E., Manuck, S. B., & Hariri, A. R. (2009). Genetic variation in components of dopamine neurotransmission impacts ventral striatal reactivity associated with impulsivity. *Molecular Psychiatry, 14*(1), 60–70.

Forsythe, R., Horowitz, J. L., Savin, N. E., & Sefton, M. (1994). Fairness in simple bargaining experiments. *Games and Economic Behavior, 6*(3), 347–369.

Gardner, W. L., Gabriel, S., & Lee, A. Y. (1999). "I" value freedom, but "we" value relationships: Self-construal priming mirrors cultural differences in judgment. *Psychological Science, 10*, 321–326.

George, L. K., Larson, D. B., Koenig, H. G., & McCullough, M. E. (2000). Spirituality and health: What we know, what we need to know. *Journal of Social and Clinical Psychology, 19*(1), 102–116.

Gould, S. J., & Lewontin, R. C. (1979). The spandrels of San Marco and the Panglossian paradigm: a critique of the adaptationist programme. *Proc. R. Soc. Lond. B, 205*(1161), 581–598.

Grossmann, I., & Jowhari, N. (2018). Cognition and the self: Attempt of an independent close replication of the effects of self-construal priming on spatial memory recall. *Journal of Experimental Social Psychology, 74,* 65–73.

Gryczynski, J., & Ward, B. W. (2011). Social norms and the relationship between cigarette use and religiosity among adolescents in the United States. *Health Education and Behavior, 38*(1), 39–48.

Haidt, J., Koller, S. H., & Dias, M. G. (1993). Affect, culture, and morality, or is it wrong to eat your dog? *Journal of Personality and Social Psychology, 65*(4), 613.

Halldorsdottir, T., & Binder, E. B. (2017). Gene × environment interactions: from molecular mechanisms to behavior. *Annual Review of Psychology, 68,* 215–241.

Hankin, B. L., Nederhof, E., Oppenheimer, C. W., Jenness, J., Young, J. F., Abela, J. R. Z., . . . & Oldehinkel, A. J. (2011). Differential susceptibility in youth: evidence that 5-HTTLPR x positive parenting is associated with positive affect "for better and worse." *Translational Psychiatry, 1*(10), e44.

Heine, S. J., Kitayama, S., Lehman, D., Takata, T., Ide, E., Leung, C., & Matsumoto, H. (2001). Divergent consequences of success and failure in Japan and North America: An investigation of self-improving motivations and malleable selves. *Journal of Personality and Social Psychology, 81,* 599–615.

Heinz, A., Haszler, A., Keidel, C., Moldenhauer, S., Benedictus, R., & Miller, W. S. (2000). Recent development in aluminium alloys for aerospace applications. *Materials Science and Engineering: A, 280*(1), 102–107.

Henrich, J., Boyd, R., Bowles, S., Camerer, C., Fehr, E., Gintis, H., . . . & Henrich, N. S. (2005). "Economic man" in cross-cultural perspective: Behavioral experiments in 15 small-scale societies. *Behavioral and Brain Sciences, 28*(6), 795–815.

Herskovits, M. J. (1948). *Man and His Works: The Science of Cultural Anthropology.* New York: Knopf.

(1955). *Cultural Anthropology.* New York: Alfred A. Knopf, Inc. Ltd.

Hofstede, G. (1984). Cultural dimensions in management and planning. *Asia Pacific Journal of Management, 1*(2), 81–99.

Hong, Y.-Y., Morris, M. W., Chiu, C.-Y., & Benet-Martinez, V. (2000). Multicultural minds: A dynamic constructivist approach to culture and cognition. *American Psychologist, 55,* 709–720.

Hurley, T. D., & Edenberg, H. J. (2012). Genes encoding enzymes involved in ethanol metabolism. *Alcohol Research: Current Reviews, 34*(3), 339.

Ishii, K., Kim, H. S., Sasaki, J. Y., Shinada, M., & Kusumi, I. (2014). Culture modulates sensitivity to the disappearance of facial expressions associated with serotonin transporter polymorphism (5-HTTLPR). *Culture and Brain, 2,* 72–88.

Ishii, K., Miyamoto, Y., Mayama, K., & Niedenthal, P. M. (2011). When your smile fades away: Cultural differences in sensitivity to the disappearance of smiles. *Social Psychological and Personality Science, 2*(5), 516–522.

Jiang, C., Varnum, M. E., Hou, Y., & Han, S. (2014). Distinct effects of self-construal priming on empathic neural responses in Chinese and Westerners. *Social Neuroscience, 9*(2), 130–138.

Jiang, Y., Bachner-Melman, R., Chew, S. H., & Ebstein, R. P. (2015). Dopamine D4 receptor gene and religious affiliation correlate with dictator game altruism in males and not females: evidence for gender-sensitive gene × culture interaction. *Frontiers in Neuroscience, 9,* 338.

Joireman, J. A., Needham, T. L., & Cummings, A. L. (2002). Relationships between dimensions of attachment and empathy. *North American Journal of Psychology, 4*(1), 63–80.

Jokela, M., Lehtimäki, T., & Keltikangas-Järvinen, L. (2007). The serotonin receptor 2A gene moderates the influence of parental socioeconomic status on adulthood harm avoidance. *Behavior Genetics, 37*(4), 567–574.

Kan, K.-J., Wicherts, J. M., Dolan, C. V., & van der Maas, H. L. J. (2013). On the nature and nurture of intelligence and specific cognitive abilities: The more heritable, the more culture dependent. *Psychological Science, 24,* 2420–2428.

Kim, B. Y., Butt, S. A., Chen, X., Jeng, S. J. J., Nayfeh, H. M., & Wehella-Gamage, D. (2008). U.S. Patent Application No. 11/616,730.

Kim, H., & Markus, H. R. (1999). Deviance or uniqueness, harmony or conformity? A cultural analysis. *Journal of Personality and Social Psychology, 77*(4), 785.

Kim, H., Nasiri, K., & Sasaki, J. Y. (2017). Cultural and genetic influences on emotion: The role of motivational processes in gene–culture interactions. In A. Church (Ed.) *Personality Across Cultures.* Santa Barbara: Praeger.

Kim, H. S., & Sasaki, J. Y. (2014). Cultural neuroscience: Biology of the mind in cultural context. *Annual Review of Psychology, 64*, 487–514.

Kim, H. S., Sherman, D. K., Mojaverian, T., Sasaki, J. Y., Park, J., Suh, E. M., & Taylor, S. E. (2011). Gene–culture interaction: Oxytocin receptor polymorphism (OXTR) and emotion regulation. *Social Psychological and Personality Science, 2*, 665–672.

Kim, H. S., Sherman, D. K., Sasaki, J. Y., Xu, J., Chu, T. Q., Ryu, C., Suh, E. M., Graham, K., & Taylor, S. E. (2010a). Culture, distress, and oxytocin receptor polymorphism (OXTR) interact to influence emotional support seeking. *Proceedings of the National Academy of Sciences, 107*, 15717–15721.

Kim, H. S., Sherman, D. K., & Taylor, S. E. (2008). Culture and social support. *American Psychologist, 63*, 518–526.

Kim, H. S., Sherman, D. K., Taylor, S. E., Sasaki, J. Y., Chu, T. Q., Ryu, C., et al. (2010b). Culture, the serotonin receptor polymorphism (5-HTR1A) and locus of attention. *Social Cognitive and Affective Neuroscience, 5*, 212–218.

Kitayama, S. (2002). Culture and basic psychological processes – toward a system view of culture: comment on Oyserman et al. (2002). *Psychological Bulletin, 128*(1), 89–96.

Kitayama, S., & Cohen, D. (Eds.). (2010). *Handbook of Cultural Psychology.* Guilford Press.

Kitayama, S., King, A., Yoon, C., Tompson, S., Huff, S., & Liberzon, I. (2014). The dopamine D4 receptor gene (DRD4) moderates cultural difference in independent versus interdependent social orientation. *Psychological Science, 25*, 1169–1177.

Kitayama, S., Markus, H. R., & Matsumoto, H. (1995). Culture, self, and emotion: A cultural perspective on "self-conscious" emotions.

Knafo, A., Israel, S., & Ebstein, R. P. (2011). Heritability of children's prosocial behavior and differential susceptibility to parenting by variation in the dopamine receptor D4 gene. *Development and Psychopathology, 23*(1), 53–67.

Kosfeld, M., Heinrichs, M., Zak, P. J., Fischbacher, U., & Fehr, E. (2005). Oxytocin increases trust in humans. *Nature, 435*(7042), 673.

Kraus, M. W., Piff, P. K., & Keltner, D. (2011). Social class as culture: The convergence of resources and rank in the social realm. *Current Directions in Psychological Science, 20*(4), 246–250.

Kuhnen, U., & Oyserman, D. (2002). Thinking about the self influences thinking in general: Cognitive consequences of salient self-concept. *Journal of Experimental Social Psychology, 38*, 492–499.

LeClair, J., Janusonis, S., & Kim, H. S. (2014). Gene–culture interactions: a multi-gene approach. *Culture and Brain, 2*(2), 122–140.

LeClair, J., Sasaki, J. Y., Ishii, K., Shinada, M., & Kim, H. S. (2016). Gene–culture interaction: Influence of culture and oxytocin receptor gene (OXTR) polymorphism on loneliness. *Culture and Brain, 4*(1), 21–37.

Lesch, K. P., Bengel, D., Heils, A., Sabol, S. Z., Greenberg, B. D., Petri, S., . . . & Murphy, D. L. (1996). Association of anxiety-related traits with a polymorphism in the serotonin transporter gene regulatory region. *Science, 274*(5292), 1527–1531.

Leung, A. K.-Y., & Cohen, D. (2011). Within- and between-culture variation: Individual differences and the cultural logics of honor, face, and dignity cultures. *Journal of Personality and Social Psychology, 100*, 507–526. doi: 10.1037/a0022151

Li, D., & He, L. (2007). Meta-analysis supports association between serotonin transporter (5-HTT) and suicidal behavior. *Molecular Psychiatry, 12*(1), 47.

Luo, S., Ma, Y., Liu, Y., Li, B., Wang, C., Shi, Z., . . . & Han, S. (2015). Interaction between oxytocin receptor polymorphism and interdependent culture values on human empathy. *Social Cognitive and Affective Neuroscience, 10*(9), 1273–1281.

Mackie, D. M. & Smith, E. R. (2014). Intergroup emotions. In J. Dovidio & J. Simpson (Eds.) *APA Handbook of Personality and Social Psychology* (Volume II: Interpersonal Relationships and Group Processes, pp. 263–294). APA Press.

Mackie, D. M., Smith, E. R. & Ray, D. G. (2008). Intergroup emotions and intergroup relations. *Personality and Social Psychology Compass, 2*, 1866–1880.

Manuck, S. B. (2011). Delay discounting covaries with childhood socioeconomic status as a function of genetic variation in the dopamine D4 receptor (DRD4). *Society for Research in Child Development, Montreal, Quebec, Canada.*

Markus, H. R., & Kitayama, S. (1991). Culture and the self: Implications for cognition, emotion, and motivation. *Psychological Review, 98*(2), 224.
   (1998). The cultural psychology of personality. *Journal of Cross-Cultural Psychology, 29*(1), 63–87.

Masuda, T., & Nisbett, R. E. (2001). Attending holistically versus analytically: comparing the context sensitivity of Japanese and Americans. *Journal of Personality and Social Psychology, 81*(5), 922.

Matsumoto, D., Takeuchi, S., Andayani, S., Kouznetsova, N., & Krupp, D. (1998). The contribution of individualism vs. collectivism to cross-national differences in display rules. *Asian Journal of Social Psychology, 1*(2), 147–165.

Matsumoto, D., Yoo, S. H., Hirayama, S., & Petrova, G. (2005). Development and validation of a measure of display rule knowledge: the display rule assessment inventory. *Emotion, 5*(1), 23.

Matsumoto, D., Yoo, S. H., & Nakagawa, S. (2008). Culture, emotion regulation, and adjustment. *Journal of Personality and Social Psychology, 94*(6), 925.

McCullough, M. E., Hoyt, W. T., Larson, D. B., Koenig, H. G., & Thoresen, C. (2000). Religious involvement and mortality: a meta-analytic review. *Health Psychology, 19*(3), 211.

Meaney, M. J. (2017). Epigenetics and the biology of gene× environment interactions. In *Gene-Environment Transactions in Developmental Psychopathology* (pp. 59–94). Springer, Cham.

Mesquita, B., & Walker, R. (2003). Cultural differences in emotions: A context for interpreting emotional experiences. *Behaviour Research and Therapy, 41*(7), 777–793.

Meyer-Lindenberg, A., & Weinberger, D. R. (2006). Intermediate phenotypes and genetic mechanisms of psychiatric disorders. *Nature Reviews Neuroscience, 7*(10), 818.

Mifflin, H. (2000). *The American Heritage Dictionary of the English Language*. New York.

Miller, G. (2013). The promise and perils of oxytocin. *Science, 339*(6117), 267–269.

Mischel, W., & Shoda, Y. (1995). A cognitive-affective system theory of personality: Reconceptualizing situations, dispositions, dynamics, and invariance in personality structure. Psychological Review, *102*(2), 246–268.

Miyamoto, Y., Nisbett, R. E., & Masuda, T. (2006). Culture and the physical environment: Holistic versus analytic perceptual affordances. *Psychological Science, 17*(2), 113–119.

Monroe, S. M., & Simons, A. D. (1991). Diathesis-stress theories in the context of life stress research: implications for the depressive disorders. *Psychological Bulletin, 110*(3), 406.

Morrell, F. (1961). Electrophysiological contributions to the neural basis of learning. *Physiological Reviews, 41*(3), 443–494.

Mrazek, A. J., Chiao, J. Y., Blizinsky, K. D., Lun, J., & Gelfand, M. J. (2013). The role of culture–gene coevolution in morality judgment: Examining the interplay between tightness–looseness and allelic variation of the serotonin transporter gene. Culture and Brain, 1(2–4), 100–117.

Mullins, N., Power, R. A., Fisher, H. L., Hanscombe, K. B., Euesden, J., Iniesta, R., . . . & Uher, R. (2016). Polygenic interactions with environmental adversity in the aetiology of major depressive disorder. *Psychological Medicine, 46*(4), 759–770.

Na, J., Grossman, I., Varnum, M. E. W., Kitayama, S., Gonzalez, R., & Nisbett, R. E. (2010). Cultural differences are not always reducible to individual differences. *Proceedings of the National Academy of Sciences, 107*, 6192–6197.

Naumova, O. Y., Hein, S., Suderman, M., Barbot, B., Lee, M., Raefski, A., . . . & Grigorenko, E. L. (2016). Epigenetic patterns modulate the connection between developmental dynamics of parenting and offspring psychosocial adjustment. *Child Development, 87*(1), 98–110.

Nisbett, R. E., Peng, K., Choi, I., & Norenzayan, A. (2001). Culture and systems of thought: Holistic versus analytic cognition. *Psychological Review, 108*, 291–310.

Oak, J. N., Oldenhof, J., & Van Tol, H. H. M. (2000). The dopamine D4 receptor: One decade of research. *European Journal of Pharmacology, 405*(1), 303–327.

Odling-Smee, F. J., Laland, K. N., & Feldman, M. W. (2003). Niche Construction: The Neglected Process in Evolution (Monographs in Population Biology No. 37). Princeton University Press.

Ogilvie, A. D., Battersby, S., Fink, G., Harmar, A. J., Goodwin, G. M., Bubb, V. J., & Smith, C. D. (1996). Polymorphism in serotonin transporter gene associated with susceptibility to major depression. *The Lancet, 347* (9003), 731–733.

Oishi, S. (2010). The psychology of residential mobility: Implications for the self, social relationships, and well-being. *Perspectives on Psychological Science, 5*(1), 5–21.

Osinsky, R., Reuter, M., Küpper, Y., Schmitz, A., Kozyra, E., Alexander, N., & Hennig, J. (2008). Variation in the serotonin transporter gene modulates selective attention to threat. *Emotion, 8*(4), 584.

Oyserman, D., & Lee, S. W. S. (2008). Does culture influence what and how we think? Effects of priming individualism and collectivism. *Psychological Bulletin, 134*, 311–342.

Panicker, V., Saravanan, P., Vaidya, B., Evans, J., Hattersley, A. T., Frayling, T. M., & Dayan, C. M. (2009). Common variation in the DIO2 gene predicts baseline psychological well-being and response to combination thyroxine plus triiodothyronine therapy in hypothyroid patients. *The Journal of Clinical Endocrinology and Metabolism, 94*(5), 1623–1629.

Pluess, M., & Belsky, J. (2009). Differential susceptibility to rearing experience: The case of childcare. *Journal of Child Psychology and Psychiatry, 50*(4), 396–404.

(2010). Differential susceptibility to parenting and quality child care. *Developmental Psychology, 46*(2), 379.

(2012). Conceptual issues in psychiatric gene-environment interaction research. *American Journal of Psychiatry, 169*(2), 222–223.

Rodrigues, S. M., Saslow, L. R., Garcia, N., John, O. P., Keltner, D. (2009). Oxytocin receptor genetic variation relates to empathy and stress reactivity in humans. *Proceedings of the National Academy of Sciences, 106*, 21437–21441.

Rothbart, M. K., & Ahadi, S. A. (1994). Temperament and the development of personality. *Journal of Abnormal Psychology, 103*(1), 55.

Rothbart, M. K., Posner, M. I., & Hershey, K. L. (2006). Temperament, attention, and developmental psychopathology. *Developmental Psychopathology, 2*, 465–501.

Rothbaum, F., Weisz, J., Pott, M., Miyake, K., & Morelli, G. (2000). Attachment and culture: Security in the United States and Japan. *American Psychologist, 55*(10), 1093.

Rubinstein, M., Phillips, T. J., Bunzow, J. R., Falzone, T. L., Dziewczapolski, G., Zhang, G.,... Chester, J. A. (1997). Mice lacking dopamine D4 receptors are supersensitive to ethanol, cocaine, and methamphetamine. *Cell, 90*(6), 991–1001.

Rutherford, S. L. (2000). From genotype to phenotype: buffering mechanisms and the storage of genetic information. *Bioessays, 22*(12), 1095–1105.

Rutter, M., Moffitt, T. E., & Caspi, A. (2006). Gene–environment interplay and psychopathology: Multiple varieties but real effects. *Journal of Child Psychology and Psychiatry, 47*(3–4), 226–261.

Sasaki, J. Y., & Kim, H. S. (2017). Nature, nurture, and their interplay: A review of cultural neuroscience. *Journal of Cross-Cultural Psychology, 48*, 4–22.

Sasaki, J. Y., Kim, H. S., Mojaverian, T., Kelley, L. D. S., Park, I. Y., & Janušonis, S. (2013). Religion priming differentially increases prosocial behavior among variants of the dopamine D4 receptor (DRD4) gene. *Social Cognitive and Affective Neuroscience, 8*, 209–215.

Sasaki, J. Y., & Kim, H. S. (2011). At the intersection of culture and religion: A cultural analysis of religion's implications for secondary control and social affiliation. *Journal of Personality and Social Psychology, 101*(2), 401.

Schild, A. H., Nader, I. W., Pietschnig, J., & Voracek, M. (2014). Ethnicity moderates the association between 5-HTTLPR and national suicide rates. *Archives of Suicide Research, 18*(1), 1–13.

Schmitt, J. A., Jorissen, B. L., Sobczak, S., van Boxtel, M. P., Hogervorst, E., Deutz, N. E., et al. (2000). Tryptophan depletion impairs memory consolidation but improves focused attention in healthy young volunteers. *Journal of Psychopharmacology*, 14, 21–9.

Segall, M. H., Lonner, W. J., & Berry, J. W. (1998). Cross-cultural psychology as a scholarly discipline: On the flowering of culture in behavioral research. *American Psychologist, 53*(10), 1101.

Seligman, M. E., & Csikszentmihalyi, M. (2000). Positive psychology: An introduction. *American Psychologist, 55*(1), 5–14.

Shariff, A. F., & Norenzayan, A. (2007). God is watching you: Priming god concepts increases prosocial behavior in an anonymous economic game. *Psychological Science, 18*, 803–809.

Shariff, A. F., Willard, A. K., Andersen, T., & Norenzayan, A. (2016). Religious priming: A meta-analysis with a focus on prosociality. *Personality and Social Psychology Review, 20*(1), 27–48.

Sheng, F., Liu, Y., Zhou, B., Zhou, W., & Han, S. (2013). Oxytocin modulates the racial bias in neural responses to others' suffering. *Biological Psychology, 92*(2), 380–386.

Shweder, R. A. (1991). *Thinking through Cultures: Expeditions in Cultural Psychology.* Harvard University Press.

Singelis, T. M. (1994). The measurement of independent and interdependent self-construals. *Personality and Social Psychology Bulletin, 20*(5), 580–591.

Snibbe, A. C., & Markus, H. R. (2005). You can't always get what you want: educational attainment, agency, and choice. *Journal of Personality and Social Psychology, 88*(4), 703.

Staub, E. (1978). *Positive Social Behavior and Morality, Volume 1: Social and Personal Influences.* Academic Press.

Stein, M. B., Schork, N. J., & Gelernter, J. (2008). Gene-by-environment (serotonin transporter and childhood maltreatment) interaction for anxiety sensitivity, an intermediate phenotype for anxiety disorders. *Neuropsychopharmacology, 33*(2), 312.

Stice, E., Yokum, S., Burger, K., Epstein, L., & Smolen, A. (2012). Multilocus genetic composite reflecting dopamine signaling capacity predicts reward circuitry responsivity. *The Journal of Neuroscience, 32*, 10093–10100.

Stright, A. D., Gallagher, K. C., & Kelley, K. (2008). Infant temperament moderates relations between maternal parenting in early childhood and children's adjustment in first grade. *Child Development, 79*(1), 186–200.

Suh, E. M. (2002). Culture, identity consistency, and subjective well-being. *Journal of Personality and Social Psychology, 83*(6), 1378.

Taylor, S. E., Sherman, D. K., Kim, H. S., Jarcho, J., Takagi, K., & Dunagan, M. S. (2004). Culture and social support: Who seeks it and why? *Journal of Personality and Social Psychology, 87*(3), 354.

Timberlake, D. S., Rhee, S. H., Haberstick, B. C., Hopfer, C., Ehringer, M., Lessem, J. M., ... & Hewitt, J. K. (2006). The moderating effects of religiosity on the genetic and environmental determinants of smoking initiation. *Nicotine and Tobacco Research, 8*(1), 123–133.

Tishkoff, S. A., & Kidd, K. K. (2004). Implications of biogeography of human populations for "race" and medicine. *Nature Genetics, 36*, S21–S27.

Triandis, H. C. (2001). Individualism-collectivism and personality. *Journal of Personality, 69*(6), 907–924.

U.S. Census Bureau. (2017, November) *Geographical Mobility: 2016 to 2017* (Table 1) Retrieved from www.census.gov/data/tables/2017/demo/geo graphic-mobility/cps-2017.html

van IJzendoorn, M. H., Bakermans-Kranenburg, M. J., & Mesman, J. (2008). Dopamine system genes associated with parenting in the context of daily hassles. *Genes, Brain and Behavior, 7*(4), 403–410.

Walum, H., Waldman, I. D., & Young, L. J. (2016). Statistical and methodological considerations for the interpretation of intranasal oxytocin studies. *Biological Psychiatry, 79*(3), 251–257.

Weaver, I. C., Cervoni, N., Champagne, F. A., D'Alessio, A. C., Sharma, S., Seckl, J. R., ... & Meaney, M. J. (2004). Epigenetic programming by maternal behavior. *Nature Neuroscience, 7*(8), 847.

White, C., Kelly, J. M., Shariff, A., & Norenzayan, A. (2018). Thinking about Karma and God reduces believers' selfishness in anonymous dictator games. Preprint.

Zannas, A. S., Wiechmann, T., Gassen, N. C., & Binder, E. B. (2016). Gene–stress–epigenetic regulation of FKBP5: clinical and translational implications. *Neuropsychopharmacology, 41*(1), 261.

Zhong, S., Israel, S., Shalev, I., Xue, H., Ebstein, R. P., & Chew, S. H. (2010). Dopamine D4 receptor gene associated with fairness preference in ultimatum game. *PLoS One, 5*(11), e13765.

Zuckerman, M. (1999). Diathesis-stress models. In M. Zuckerman, *Vulnerability to Psychopathology: A Biosocial Model*, pp. 3–23. Washington, DC, US: American Psychological Association.

Cambridge Elements ≡

Psychology and Culture

Kenneth D. Keith

University of San Diego

Kenneth D. Keith is author or editor of more than 160 publications
on cross-cultural psychology, quality of life, intellectual disability,
and the teaching of psychology. He was the 2017 president of the Society
for the Teaching of Psychology.

About the Series

Elements in Psychology and Culture features authoritative surveys and updates
on key topics in cultural, cross-cultural, and indigenous psychology. Authors
are internationally recognized scholars whose work is at the forefront
of their subdisciplines within the realm of psychology
and culture.

Cambridge Elements ☰

Psychology and Culture

Elements in the Series

Printed in the United States
By Bookmasters